IMAGES
of America

WRANGELL

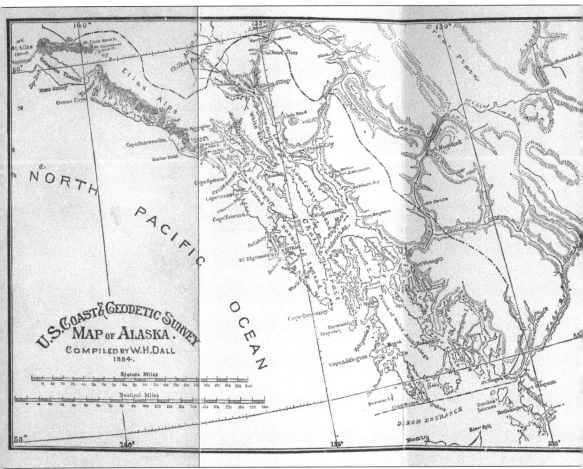

William H. Dall was one of the first American naturalists to study the interior of Alaska. He drew this map while working for the US Coast and Geodetic Survey in 1884. The map was included in a book published in 1885 by Eliza R. Scidmore, who toured Alaska and wrote about her trip in letters for the *New York Times*. Fort Wrangel, as it was spelled in those days, is center right. (Courtesy of the Irene Ingle Public Library.)

ON THE COVER: Wrangell is a town growing beyond its rude frontier beginnings in this image from around 1910. Smoke from the Willson and Sylvester sawmill rises, center, behind the cluster of buildings that mark the Chief Shakes Tribal House. Churches, shops, and homes that at first hugged the shore are beginning to climb the hills. In the foreground are buildings of another Tlingit clan, the Shustak. (Photograph by John E. Worden; courtesy of MCN.)

Bonnie Demerjian

Copyright © 2011 by Bonnie Demerjian
ISBN 978-1-5316-4945-6

Published by Arcadia Publishing
Charleston, South Carolina

Library of Congress Control Number: 2010940450

For all general information, please contact Arcadia Publishing:
Telephone 843-853-2070
Fax 843-853-0044
E-mail sales@arcadiapublishing.com
For customer service and orders:
Toll-Free 1-888-313-2665

Visit us on the Internet at www.arcadiapublishing.com

To Haig, for your unwavering support all these years.

Contents

Acknowledgments		6
Introduction		7
1.	Fort Wrangel	9
2.	Front Street	15
3.	Church, School, Hospital, and Home	35
4.	Boats	51
5.	Making a Living on Land and Sea	65
6.	The Fourth of July	79
7.	Totems	85
8.	People	99
9.	Panoramas	119
Bibliography		126
Index		127

Acknowledgments

A large number of people both living and gone have contributed to this book. I would like to thank particularly the Wrangell Museum (WM) and directors Dennis Chapman and Megan Clark for permission to utilize the museum's sizable photograph collection. That collection is the result of the donations of numerous benefactors over the years. The Friends of the Museum has also been supportive with its interest in local history and the preservation of Wrangell's past for future generations. Thanks to Tracy Churchill for assistance in accessing the museum's photographs and for sharing her detailed knowledge of its collection.

Mike and Carolyn Nore (MCN) have been most generous in offering the use of their extensive personal collection and in transforming those photographs for use in the book. Their years spent amassing archival photographs of Wrangell have resulted in an invaluable resource that has contributed immeasurably to this book.

Many in Wrangell have added their memories and photographs to make this book possible: Dick and Barbara Angerman, Fred and Merce Angerman, Leonard and Kathie Angerman, Lawrence Bahovic, Glen Barlow, Bryant and Joan Benjamin, Marge Byrd, Leonard and Lynne Campbell, Jan Churchill, Millie Grant, Lois Hope, Chris Jenkins, Greg McCormack, John Martin, Dan Nore, Dorothy Ottesen, Chuck Petticrew, Harriet Schirmer, Carol Snoddy, Harry Sundberg, and Skip and Sylvia Wells.

Thank you to Marge Byrd, Willie Eyon, Walter Moorhead, Pat Roppel, and Carol Ross for your help in editing.

City employees Dee Dee Blatchley, Kay Jabusch, Christie Jamieson, and Carl Johnson have been most helpful in locating information. I would also like to thank Steve Brown for contributing his knowledge about Wrangell's totems.

John E. Worden's excellent photographs were an important contribution to this book. He came to Wrangell in 1898 with his wife, Nina, and daughter Lynn. He was postmaster and also served as city clerk, all the while documenting Wrangell's people and places on film with artistry and empathy. His gift has allowed us to vividly experience early Wrangell, and I am deeply grateful to him. Each generation needs someone like him to capture Wrangell's present for the future. I also am indebted to his granddaughter Nina Mollhagen and great-granddaughter Nancy Mollhagen for permission to use the photographs.

Lastly, I extend my gratitude to Arcadia Publishing for offering me this chance to delve into the past of my hometown and to my editor, Laura Chaney, for her advice in bringing this book to completion.

Introduction

The city of Wrangell often introduces itself as the town that has been ruled by three nations—Russia, Britain, and the United States. In truth, earliest ownership dates from the prehistoric clan legends of the Stikine Tlingit. The Stikines were one of the most wealthy and powerful of the Tlingit tribes, numbering around 1,500 out of a total pre-contact population of 8,000 Tlingits. Legend says they migrated to the Wrangell area from the upper Stikine River, settling first on various islands near the mouth before moving to Chugan-an or Waterfall Town, today called Mill Creek. One group then moved to a Wrangell Island site now called Old Town, but it was once named Kositlan or Willow Town by its residents.

The *Dragon*, a ship from Boston, was the first in the region to trade with the Tlingit in 1799. The Stikine Tlingit mainly traded with the Russian American Company at Fort Simpson near Prince Rupert, British Columbia, until 1834 when the company, under charter from the Russian government, established a redoubt or trading post on a narrow point in Wrangell harbor. There, they intended to trade with the Tlingit for furs while expanding Russia's influence in the area in hopes of keeping the British Hudson's Bay Company from infiltrating the country.

The Stikine Tlingit held a monopoly on trade on the Stikine River. They traded with the Tahltan people upriver, exchanging shells, fish, and Western trade goods for obsidian, berries, and other items. With the arrival of the Russians, the Tlingit continued this arrangement, acting as middlemen for the lush furs of the Alaska Interior. The establishment of Redoubt St. Dionysius at Wrangell drew Tlingit to the new settlement. They built tribal houses, and by the end of the Russian era, there was estimated to be about 1,500 Tlingit living near the fort.

In 1839, the Russian government leased the fort and mainland coast to Britain's Hudson's Bay Company in return for a rental fee of 2,000 sea otter skins annually, as well as foodstuffs. The Hudson's Bay Company took over the fort the next year, renaming it Fort Stikine and establishing a small company of 20 men including 10 Hawaiians. Tense, often violent, relations between the company and Alaska Natives, fueled in part by trade in alcohol and poor management, led to closure of the fort in 1849. The British continued to trade from ships and trading posts on the Stikine River and as far inland as Telegraph Creek into the 20th century.

Wrangell was a trading center during its next phase as an outfitting and transportation hub for three gold rushes. The first, the Stikine rush, was triggered by the discovery of gold on the Stikine River in 1861. Buck Choquette, a French-Canadian prospector and veteran of earlier rushes, located placer deposits on a Stikine River gravel bar with the help of Tlingit guides. The ensuing rush proved to be only a minor flurry but brought prospectors to Wrangell and the river for several years. Gold was found again in the Cassiar District of British Columbia in 1872, spurring another round of men making their way through Wrangell. They arrived in early spring on ocean-going steamers, then disembarked with their bulky outfits that had to be transported to the mouth of the Stikine River. Then, they either waited for the ice to break up before heading upriver in canoes and steamers or trekked over river ice and snow to the gold fields in central

British Columbia. Most miners returned for the winter, either heading south or remaining in Wrangell where most whiled away the dark months in cards and drink.

The onset of the Klondike rush brought the Army back to reoccupy Fort Wrangel one last time. The Stikine River was advertised as an easy route to the Klondike River in the Yukon. It proved to be far from easy and most stampeders who attempted to reach the gold fields from the Stikine River and overland returned in discouragement to try another way or give up. With other routes proving more accessible, Wrangell's boom faded and the Army left for Skagway in 1900. Wrangell, however, continued to be a support center for northern British Columbia until the 1950s.

In between these boom times, Wrangell, or Fort Wrangel as it was then known, sank back into somnolence. Tourists began arriving in the 1880s to view the many totem poles. Some few who came for gold ended up staying for a lifetime and helped the town settle into maturity by establishing stores and service businesses. In 1903, Fort Wrangel incorporated and took on a standardized new name: Wrangell. Businesses such as fishing, salmon canneries, and sawmills sprang up in the late 1890s and the town's economy began to stabilize. With the formation of the Tongass National Forest in 1906, timber sales increased, so that by the 1980s, Wrangell was called the lumber capital of Alaska. Salmon canning, shrimp, and crab processing continued to support the economy though the 20th century.

Two fires have destroyed Wrangell's business section so that a large number of Wrangell's historic buildings were turned to ashes. Many others simply decayed. Following the most recent fire in 1952, the waterfront was greatly changed and enlarged with fill so that the shoreline of the past is often difficult to envision. Still, a stroll down Front Street can reveal some of the buildings of the city's past, although a number are greatly altered. Those that have disappeared and the people who lived and worked in them now exist only in the photographs that follow.

One
FORT WRANGEL

Upon its purchase of Alaska, the US government placed the territory under control of the War Department with the US Army as the sole authority. Six posts were established in the territory, and one of the chief ones was Fort Wrangel. Troops arrived on May 5, 1868, and began constructing the post, named after Baron Ferdinand von Wrangell, a Russian American Company commander and governor of Russian America. The men began clearing ground on a point of land with clear views of both the straits and the mouth of the Stikine. By 1870, however, the War Department found that its Alaska posts were too expensive and all except Sitka were closed. The buildings were sold to local entrepreneur William "King" Lear for $600. Lear attempted to charge the Army rent when the post was remanned in 1874 during the Cassiar rush, but the sale was determined to be invalid. The Army was brought to Fort Wrangel this second time to help control liquor smuggling and keep order, but again in 1877, despite objections from Fort Wrangel's citizens, the Army withdrew from Alaska and Fort Wrangel was evacuated. The rapid influx of prospectors at the time of the Klondike Gold Rush brought back the Army one last time in May 1898 to help maintain order, but on this occasion, they found Fort Wrangel a more settled community. The beginnings of civil law in the form of the Harrison Bill, passed in 1884, had provided for courts and a governor. The lawlessness of early decades was over, leaving the troops with little to do. In May 1900, they were transferred to Skagway. The buildings of the fort were used for federal government offices, schools, and other public services until they were either torn down or moved. Today, the federal building, built on the site of the courthouse, continues Fort Wrangel's tradition of government use.

This unsophisticated drawing, dated August 21, 1876, depicts the early American fort. It was built sometime during 1868 to 1869 and abandoned only two years later, to be occupied again in 1874. A large building and dock with a ship in the center may indicate William McKinnon's store, one of Fort Wrangel's first businesses. Native canoes line the shore. (*New Dominion Monthly*, September–October 1877; courtesy of MCN.)

In this photograph from about 1910 are the remains of the Russian American Company's Fort Dionysius. The redoubt was described in 1834 as constructed of boards fastened to poles about six feet high with huts of cedar bark within it for shelter. It stood on a small island in the harbor (near today's Marine Bar) and was accessible by a footbridge. It was dependent for water on a small stream nearby that was vulnerable to Native interference. (Courtesy of MCN.)

After the Army departed in 1877, Fort Wrangel and the rest of Alaska fell under the jurisdiction of the US government's Treasury Department with the Revenue Cutter Service providing a modicum of law. The Organic Act of 1884 created civil government for the territory and the fort buildings were used as government offices. Several fort buildings, including the two-story building at center, were also used as school quarters by Presbyterian missionaries who had begun work with the Alaska Natives in 1877. The fort's stockade is still in place here, as is the blockhouse to the right of the hospital. It was built by the Hudson's Bay Company and incorporated into the fort. In 1872 and 1873, the Cassiar Gold Rush brought commercial activity to Fort Wrangel. Entrepreneur William "King" Lear built a warehouse and wharf on the right. By the late 1880s, as seen here, Fort Wrangel was again mostly a Native settlement. Note Mount Dewey shorn of trees from the construction of the fort. (Photograph by D.G. Davidson; courtesy of MCN.)

The fort's 12-foot-high stockade with its two great gates is gone in this photograph taken in the early 1890s. A fence surrounds the home of pioneer businessman Rufus Sylvester, center. The two-story building in the center was originally a hospital, then Alaska Native school and courthouse. When the Army first occupied the fort, the two-story house on the left was the officer's quarters. Later, it was the Customs House. (Photograph by Edward or William Partridge; courtesy of MCN.)

Many soldiers at Fort Wrangel were veterans of the Civil War. Pictured are three of the 63 men from Company H of the 14th US Infantry sent here during the Klondike rush. Soldiers were frequently blamed for degrading the Stikine people through drink and debauchery. (Photograph by Otto Goetze; courtesy of MCN.)

This building was constructed as a barracks. From 1882 until 1888, it was used as the Thlingit Training Academy, a boys' school run by Presbyterian missionary Fanny Kellogg Young. This image from 1898 shows a rooftop sign for the *Stikine River Journal*, published briefly in the building from a cell in the blockhouse. Following the 1906 fire, the *Wrangell Sentinel* was also printed from this building. (Courtesy of the WM.)

A steamship is tied at the McCormack Dock in this photograph from the 1890s. The killer whale totem with a missing dorsal fin was moved to the fort grounds following the 1906 fire. It is probably the same figure pictured in earlier photographs of a Tlingit house. The building on the right is the Customs House with other former fort office structures and the Customs warehouse. (Courtesy of MCN.)

By 1908, the Native school building, right, was no longer needed because a new school for Alaska Natives had been constructed in 1906. The building was torn down in 1920, and a new one accommodating all federal functions was completed in 1921. Leonard Campbell's grandfather, Hiram, was the US deputy marshal at the time of the building's construction and his family lived upstairs. (Photograph by John E. Worden; courtesy of MCN.)

This is the federal building built in 1921 to replace the old hospital-school-courthouse. The original fort property of about two acres included officers' quarters, hospital, blockhouse, garden, barracks, kitchens, and bakery, all surrounded by a stockade. This land is still owned by the US government. (Courtesy of Leonard and Lynne Campbell.)

Two

FRONT STREET

Front Street, once called Main Street, has always been Wrangell's business center on its north end, while the southern waterfront was originally the Native section. As Tlingit families made the gradual move to Fort Wrangel, they established tribal houses around the harbor with the Nan ya yii and other high caste tribes settling on Shakes Island. The beach served to connect houses and fort, but no walkway was constructed until 1883. As in early communities everywhere, refuse was thrown outside the houses and littered the beach. Visitors to the town never failed to comment on the mud and general disorder of the beachfront.

Gradually, more boardwalks, and then plank streets extended the length of the business district, but it was not until 1944 that the street was paved. With the destruction of most waterside businesses in the 1952 fire, fill was brought in to widen the business district. Buildings on the former waterfront were now established on firm ground rather than on pilings over the beach. Although Front Street stores turned their backs on the beach, a series of wharves, floats, canneries, and cold storage plants maintained the connection of Wrangell's business and community life to the ocean.

The new-filled ground, in addition to the disappearance of pre-fire buildings and the remodeling of existing structures, makes it difficult to envision early Front Street. Thankfully, a few relics survive—the Patenaude building (later Millie's) and the Greif building (later Norris' Gift Shop)—to help orient us today. And, unlike many town centers that have been drained of life by malls and big-box stores, Front Street remains the vital commercial heart of Wrangell.

Following the Cassiar rush, Fort Wrangel dwindled again. Chinese miners were the only ones working the claims. During the winter, they lived in the beached riverboat seen in both photographs. Alaska's economy began to improve in the late 1880s as canneries and a sawmill were established along with tourism. The number of vessels in Alaska increased, carrying gold, fish, lumber, and mining equipment, as well as passengers and tourists. Missionary Sheldon Jackson and John Muir encouraged visitors. Fort Wrangel became one stop on a standard cruise; it took 30 days and cost $98 from Seattle. As seen below, the town's appearance often failed to impress. Missionary Carrie Willard said, "Wrangell may be described as a mudhole and a wharf." At the time these 1880s images were taken, many of the log houses stood empty. (Above, courtesy of the WM; below, photographer George M. Weister; courtesy of MCN.)

Front Street is pictured here about 1888. The buildings on the left were situated where Angerman's stores are today. There were no saloons, as liquor was outlawed in Alaska, though brewing hooch was common. The first boardwalk, built in front of today's Totem Bar, was constructed in 1883. The Alaska Native section ran south from where the Taylor building is today around the inner harbor. (Photograph by Edward De Groff; courtesy of MCN.)

Cows wander the north end of Front Street in this photograph taken before the fire of 1906 destroyed most of the buildings seen here. A sign on the two-story building next to the drugstore advertises the way to the opera house. The small structure at the far end of the street was the old fort stable. (Courtesy of the WM.)

Fort Wrangel was quiet between the Cassiar and Klondike rushes. Seen here is lower Front Street and a part of the Native village looking north. Note the blanket covering the canoe on the lower left to keep the wood from drying and splitting. The Presbyterian Church is at the far left center. Tourists were fascinated with the totems and the Tlingits' daily lives, sometimes even wandering uninvited into homes to observe them. (Courtesy of MCN.)

Only a few years later in 1898, this same area has exploded with tent stores on both sides of the street. Businesses hoped to attract and entertain prospectors headed up the Stikine River to Glenora and the overland route to Teslin Lake, then on to the Yukon River and the Klondike fields. (Photograph by Stephen Joseph Thompson; courtesy of MCN.)

Log houses have been succeeded by cedar shakes and milled lumber in this view of south Wrangell. A visitor in 1896 counted 139 houses with another 26 in Foreign Town, which was north of the fort, as well as one courthouse, a jail, a Customs House, a sawmill, a brewery, a lodging house and saloon, one restaurant, a shoemaker's shop, and three stores. The Presbyterian Church's steeple is on the far right. (Photograph by V.D. Willson; courtesy of MCN.)

Looking north at Front Street around 1900, we see that frame structures have now replaced tent-frame stores. A boardwalk extends as far south as the Beihl building (today's Chamber of Commerce site). On the right is a sample store where traveling salesmen would entice buyers with their wares. Bruno Greif's saloon (later the Norris building) is visible in the center rear. (Courtesy of MCN.)

Red Men's Hall, Wrangell, Alaska. Photo by Worden.

The Improved Order of Red Men was the first fraternal organization in Wrangell. They formed in 1904, and during that year, Bruno Greif donated a site on Front Street (the former Alley Cat) for a hall. They operated a theater in the building and many public gatherings took place here. In 1912, the Red Men established the town cemetery and built a wharf to unload coffins. (Photograph by V.D. Willson; courtesy of MCN.)

In 1908, dentist Dr. James H. Wheeler constructed this building. The lower floor was a drugstore with medical offices above and it was known as Wrangell Drug. It later served as an office for Dr. Dawes, then as office and private hospital for Dr. Pigg. In 1928, it was renamed Wheeler Drugs. Today, it is part of the Totem Bar. (Courtesy of the WM.)

The Alert Fire Department was organized in 1903, but lack of equipment and a water shortage meant that when a fire started in the Pioneer Hotel (Buness Brothers), it quickly spread. Bucket lines failed to halt the blaze. Several small buildings were torn down near the St. Michaels' Trading Company (near Ottesen's today) and the fire was finally halted. The Pioneer Hotel itself suffered minor damage and can be seen standing center left in the lower photograph. John G. Grant, owner of the Pioneer, reopened one month later and began reconstruction of his other property, the Fort Wrangel Hotel. John Worden, who lost both house and business, took the bottom picture the day after on March 24, 1906. Within a year, much of the district was again in business. (Below, photograph by John E. Worden; both courtesy of the WM.)

Farquahar Matheson began his career in the north as an agent for the Hudson's Bay Company before building a store in Wrangell in 1907. At first, the post office and cable office occupied the west end of the building and the store took up the east portion. Matheson became a prominent member of the community and was serving as mayor at the time of his death in 1919. (Courtesy of MCN.)

Sled dogs were brought to Wrangell after the Klondike rush. A good sled dog sold for $50 in 1913, the approximate date this photograph was taken. They hauled freight, such as these bags of coal, which would be unloaded on the McCormack Dock. The stores shown are the Matheson Store and the Pioneer Hotel. (Photograph by Fred Cheney; courtesy of the WM.)

In 1909, Shakes Avenue was lined with businesses and homes, many belonging to Alaska Native families. To the right is a floating boardwalk that led to Shakes' Island. On the right are tourists on their way to visit the clan house there. Trident Seafoods now occupies the land where all the buildings on the left stood. (Courtesy of MCN.)

Three bars are visible in about 1915. The Bohemian Bar occupied the site of today's Ottesen's True Value. Down the street is the Stikine Hotel (formerly Bruno Greif's Fort Wrangel Brewery Beer Hall), and opposite from the hotel is the Tannhauser. Greif built his hall to dispense beer from his brewery across the street. Antime Lemieux bought it and it later became the Drift Inn. (Courtesy of MCN.)

Wrangell's first fire station was built in 1907 at the foot of Episcopal Street following the disastrous fire the previous year. A series of rain barrels and a fire bell were in place, but a water shortage hindered fire fighting in both 1906 and 1952. (Courtesy of MCN.)

Wrangell's second fire station, seen here, was built in 1912, replacing the earlier building. In 1914, the fire company changed its name to the Wrangell Fire Department. The fire bell rang both for fires and for a curfew set at 9:00 p.m. for everyone under the age of 16. There were different fire signals for each district—Central, North End, and Shingle Mill. (Photograph by Dorothy Ottesen; courtesy of Dorothy Ottesen.)

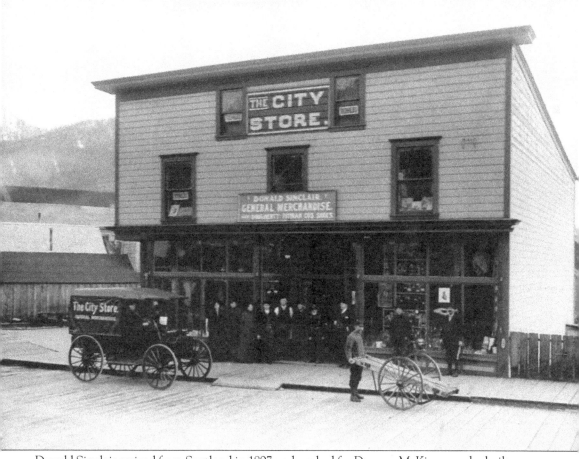

Donald Sinclair arrived from Scotland in 1897 and worked for Duncan McKinnon, who built one of Wrangell's first stores on this site. Following McKinnon's death in 1900, Sinclair opened City Store. He was an enterprising businessman who installed Wrangell's first telephone to connect his home and store in 1907. He acquired the motorized delivery wagon pictured here in 1911, and in the following year, built the first garage to house it. Handcarts, such as the one pictured here, would soon become obsolete. Those who still remember the store recall its mezzanine running around the upper floor, imitating stores in more urban areas. Sinclair operated the business, which was located on the present Elks Lodge site, until 1941. (Courtesy of MCN.)

The 75-foot-wide boardwalk was installed in 1903. By 1905, electric streetlights lined Front Street. At center left of this 1915 photograph is the Patenaude building. This has been a landmark since Leo Patenaude raised it after the 1906 fire. The city council met upstairs until the town hall was built on Church Street in 1911 (today's Senior Center). It housed Millie Grant's store for years. (Courtesy of MCN.)

The Fort Wrangel Hotel, on the site of today's Ottesen's Annex, was a three-story building before it burned in 1906. John G. Grant rebuilt it as a two-story building and added a new third story in 1924. It was advertised as a headquarters for tourists and big game hunters, with hot and cold running water in all 76 rooms. (Courtesy of the WM.)

On the far left of this image, taken about 1915, is the distinctive Greif building. Next to it is the Uhler/Nolan building, now Stikine Drug, built in 1913. It was originally a log structure housing a general merchandise store. In 1929, James Nolan purchased the building and moved his Den O' Sweets there, as well as adding a drugstore. The Engstrom (Taylor) building, center, was built in 1910. (Courtesy of MCN.)

Doctor Anna Brown Kearsley moved to Wrangell and opened this office and hospital in 1918. She led a Native health club and her office served as a US public health clinic until it was moved to a former fort building, the same used by the American Legion, in 1923. Her hospital was located where Zak's Restaurant is today. (Courtesy of the WM.)

In the 1880s, Wrangell's post office was behind the Patenaude building. It moved to the fort blockhouse and later to a small building at the north end of Front Street. By 1907, it was located in the Matheson building and then in the former Lemieux building on Cow Alley (behind Angerman's). By 1929, the post office was in the Stikine Drug building, at left, until the present federal building was constructed in 1940. (Courtesy of MCN.)

This photograph, taken from an approaching steamship, dates from the 1920s and shows oil in barrels and piles of coal on the McCormack Dock. Rails on the dock were used to transfer coal and other freight via carts to Front Street businesses. Coal was commonly used at this time for heating, although wood waste from the sawmill was also used. (Courtesy of MCN.)

In the summer of 1920, the US Army flew from New York state to Nome, Alaska, to prove that commercial airlines could deliver airmail to the north. Pictured is one of four De Havilland 4-Bs over town. They flew to Nome from Mineola, New York, stopping on Sergief Island in the delta to refuel before continuing north. All planes returned successfully to New York after flying 9,000 miles. (Courtesy of the WM.)

This 1927 photograph depicts the Columbia and Northern Fishing and Packing Company wharf, center, as well as a small floating dock. The tall building at far left was the facility belonging to the company. The wharf was located approximately where city hall is today with a walkway (today's Lynch Street) leading to it. (Courtesy of MCN.)

Dog teams delivered milk each winter using boardwalks such as this one, built in 1916. It was the forerunner of today's McKinnon Street. Another walkway to the right became today's Church Street. George Bidwell built the house in the center. To the right rear is a house built by George Sinclair, owner of the City Store. (Courtesy of the WM.)

While acting as a fur buyer and mail carrier, Walter Waters began acquiring Alaska Native artifacts and opened the Bear Totem Store (now the Arcade) in 1922. The bear totems were former grave totems from Prince of Wales Island. Waters purchased a large portion of the Shakes regalia upon the death of Shakes VI. In 1953 it was sold to the Thomas Burke Museum in Seattle. (Photograph by Otto C. Schallerer; courtesy of Greg McCormack.)

The Coliseum movie house was located on the site of the present Kadin building and was among the many structures destroyed in the 1952 fire. It was formerly the Starland Theater, owned by Sam Cunningham. He sold the building to the Gross theater chain in 1930. The transfer meant big changes for Wrangell moviegoers—talkies and soft seats. (Courtesy of the WM.)

Charles Benjamin bought this building, the former Miles Mercantile, in 1912. Benjamin had come to Wrangell in 1907. He logged, earning money to buy this store where he sold groceries, hardware, and engines. Pictured from left to right are Charles, an unidentified man, and Charles's son Lloyd Benjamin. In 1972, Lloyd, followed by his son Bryant, operated a store at a new location, now Bob's IGA. (Courtesy of Bryant Benjamin.)

The buildings seen here, from left to right, are the Bank of Alaska, Campbell Brothers Mercantile, and the fire hall. The bank's original location was in the Wrangell Hotel in 1916. The next year, this concrete building was erected. Campbell's store, owned by Ernest and Leonard Campbell, was built in 1934 on the site of St. Michael's Trading Company, founded in 1898 by Patrick. C. McCormack. Ottesen's now occupies this location. (Courtesy of Dorothy Ottesen.)

Wrangell's fire hall was replaced in 1941 by this Art Deco building in the same location. The firehouse also served as firemen's quarters, police department, and jail until the present public safety building was erected on Zimovia Highway. The building seen here was incorporated into Ottesen's store in 1987. (Photograph by Richard Ramme; courtesy of Dorothy Ottesen.)

Front Street was a tangle of wires in the 1940s. Although the buildings appear to rest on land, all those on the left were consumed in the 1952 fire as the blaze swept through the pilings on which they stood. A sign for City Meat Market, left of center, marks the old Red Men's Hall, later Roland Curtis' City Market. (Photograph by Otto C. Schallerer; courtesy of the Irene Ingle Public Library.)

The explosion of a furnace in the Wrangell Electric and Supply Company (located approximately where the Thunderbird Hotel is today) at 10:30 in the evening of March 21, 1952, quickly spread fire, destroying much of the waterfront in only four hours. Two Coast Guard cutters aided firefighters, but even that, plus one of the heaviest recorded rains falling during the fire, failed to stem the blaze. (Courtesy of the WM.)

The fire was finally brought under control at the McCormack Dock and Wrangell Cold Storage (the present City Dock area). The last building to collapse was the historic Wrangell Hotel. In all, the fire destroyed 22 buildings, including many homes. Fire chief William D. Grant estimated $1.5 million worth of damage. Valiant work by firefighters saved the upland side of the street, although the heat blistered business fronts. Dynamite was used unsuccessfully to halt the fire's spread, and it took its own toll on windows. As in the 1906 fire, low water pressure hindered firefighters. Pres. Harry Truman declared Wrangell a disaster area in April. Following the fire, Wrangell citizens considered and then rejected the idea of rebuilding over the water. The entire waterfront area was filled in 1955, forever altering the appearance of Front Street. (Courtesy of the WM.)

Three

CHURCH, SCHOOL, HOSPITAL, AND HOME

Wrangell's churches, schools, and hospitals were tightly intertwined in their formative years. The church, under the direction of Presbyterian missionaries, was largely responsible for the establishment of the first schools in the town for Natives. Philip McKay or Clah, a Tsimpsian Indian, arrived in 1876 and began conducting church services in one of the fort buildings. Shortly after, he started a small school. A letter by a soldier at the fort inspired the Presbyterian Church to send missionaries Amanda McFarland and then Rev. S. Hall Young. McFarland established a school for young women and, later, another for young men. These schools were successful in educating Alaska Native youth, but also vigorously worked to undo Tlingit culture. There were also small privately run schools for white children at this time.

Later, when the city of Wrangell was formed, the federal government continued the funding of education for Native children. The municipality supported a public school for white children. A new integrated school was built in 1930.

Besides the Presbyterian Church, a Roman Catholic mission was established, and in 1903, dissenting members of the Presbyterian Church formed St. Philip's Episcopal Church. Around the same time, a Salvation Army mission was formed in Wrangell. A number of other churches have been added through the years.

Prior to 1925, there were several small hospitals in Wrangell, operated privately by doctors. In 1926, Episcopal Bishop Peter Trimble Rowe arranged for a closed hospital in Ketchikan to be moved to Wrangell. It served the town for 42 years before today's Wrangell Medical Center opened in 1968.

Wrangell's first homes were Tlingit clan houses. Early white men constructed small houses with bunks built around the walls and a central stove. As time passed, most Native homes were rebuilt with milled lumber and windows, some in elaborate Victorian style. There was a burst of homebuilding in the 1920s and 1930s by prosperous businessmen, and houses began to climb the hills behind town. Road building to the north and south beginning in the 1930s led to further housing expansion.

The original Presbyterian Church, pictured above in 1914, was begun in 1876 under the direction of Philip McKay. It was completed using lumber from Shakan in 1879 and was the first Protestant church in Alaska. This building burned in 1930 and was a complete loss, but was rebuilt the following year. The manse (below), also built in 1879, was torn down and rebuilt in 1921 by Hiram D. Campbell. Edward Ludecke, a veteran who had been present at the hoisting of the first American flag in Sitka, built the plank walk seen below in 1904 for 5¢ a foot. (Above, courtesy of Bryant Benjamin; below, photograph by John E. Worden; courtesy of the WM.)

St. Philip's Episcopal Church began in 1903 when the Rev. Henry Prosper Corser established the People's Church with Native members of his Presbyterian congregation on property donated by the Kiksadi clan. He was ordained into the Episcopal Church and served until 1934. He built a gymnasium to the left of the church and started St. Philip's Academy to educate Alaska Native youth past the eighth grade. (Courtesy of Dorothy Ottesen.)

Bishop Charles Seghers and the Rev. John Althoff founded St. Rose of Lima Catholic Church, the first Catholic parish in Alaska, in 1879. That year, a small church was built. It fell into disrepair and was demolished in 1898. A larger one was constructed in 1909. Fr. Francis Monroe added the priest's rectory/meeting hall and initiated today's landscaping during his tenure, which began in 1924. (Courtesy of the WM.)

In 1902, Klawock Salvation Army leader William Benson arrived in Wrangell. Accompanied by flags, drums, and song, the group landed, and by the end of his visit, a corps was established. Wrangell Tlingit leader William Tamaree raised funds for the Salvation Army Barracks and donated the land next to his home. The church was built in 1904 and led by Robert Smith and Chester Worthington. Wrangell served as divisional headquarters for work in Alaska and British Columbia until 1944. The barracks was located on Front Street where Hair Unlimited is today. In 1932, during the Great Depression, the Salvation Army opened a soup kitchen to provide hot lunches every day for children at the St. Philip's Gym. The church was torn down in 1987, and a new church was raised at its present location on Zimovia Highway. (Courtesy of MCN.)

After the Army left in 1877, Presbyterian missionary Sheldon Jackson established a school for Native children. Classes were held in the fort's hospital building, above left, with Amanda McFarland in charge. The building also served as a boarding house for Alaska Native girls until a new boarding home was built south of the Presbyterian Church. It burned in 1883. Fanny Kellogg started the Thlingit Training Academy for boys that same year in another former fort building, but soon after, all teachers and students were moved to Sitka. Churches provided all education in Alaska until 1884. Native students are pictured on the fort parade grounds (above) and on the porch of the school (below). Their attendance was irregular, as most spent a part of each year at fishing and hunting camps. (Above, courtesy of the WM; below, courtesy of MCN.)

The federally funded Native school was built in 1906 on the site of today's Wrangell Middle School. Incorporated towns, which Wrangell became in 1903, were allowed to establish schools and maintain them through taxation, thus a school for white children was also built in 1906. Separate education for white and Alaska Native children continued until 1923. That year, due to protests from Native parents about segregated education, Native students were moved to the public school, though initially in a separate room. From that year until 1930, the Alaska Native school was used as a high school. Both photographs date from 1908. In the image below, teacher Mrs. Pusey is seen with her class. (Above, courtesy of MCN; below, courtesy of Bryant Benjamin.)

Wrangell's first public school for white children was built on land donated by a school grant signed by Pres. Theodore Roosevelt. The public library now sits on this site. Initially, the school was built for lower grades. In 1909, ninth grade was added, and in 1917, two wings were added to provide high school rooms. Because of expanding enrollment, students made use of the Native school and even the Presbyterian Church. Prior to 1917, high school classes were held in the town hall (today's Wrangell Senior Center). Liberty Worden was the high school's first graduate, as well as the youngest student to graduate from an Alaskan high school. When a new public school was built in 1931, city hall moved into the old school. (Both courtesy of the WM.)

Maypole festivals were a tradition on the fort grounds. In 1921, Mayor John Grant declared a holiday that included a parade with floats representing periods in Wrangell history. That year, Helen Fletcher was named the May queen with flower girls Lois Wheeler, Margaret Ferguson, Billy Ferguson, Marjorie Benjamin, Beatrice Palmer, Dorothy Voss, and Juanita Rinehart. (Courtesy of the WM.)

On October 5, 1931, Wrangell's new public school opened at a cost of $50,000. It included students from first grade through high school. On opening day, elementary students walked from their old school carrying books, tablets, and a flag. Elementary rooms were downstairs, while the upper grades were on the second floor. This building was razed in 1985 when the present high school was built. (Courtesy of the WM.)

In 1932, the Wrangell Institute opened as an industrial high school with about 75 students. The school eventually filled 19 buildings. In 1947, the Mount Edgecumbe boarding school opened in Sitka and the institute's high school students were transferred there. In the early 1960s, ninth grade was again added at the institute. The school began to stress academic rather than vocational classes. The school closed in 1975, and all the buildings have been razed. Although there was a gravel road built in the 1920s to the institute site, its rough condition encouraged service by boat until the 1960s. A dock built in 1938 by the Civil Conservation Corps allowed students and freight to be delivered directly to the school. (Both courtesy of the WM.)

When the Arthur Yates hospital, maintained by the Episcopal Board of Missions in Ketchikan, was slated to be closed, Episcopal Bishop Peter Trimble Rowe arranged for the hospital to be moved to Wrangell. The hospital opened in April 1926. Two years later the U.S. government established a public health service in the hospital for seamen, officers of merchant vessels, the Coast Guard, and lighthouse keepers. The hospital had ten private rooms, three wards, and one of only two passenger elevators in Alaska. When it opened, the hospital served not only Wrangell, but also the west coast of Prince of Wales Island, Petersburg, and the Cassiar District. In 1926 ward beds were $3.50 and private rooms were $5.00 a day. During the years the hospital was in service, many a baby was born there, delivered by Dr. John Bangeman. The Bishop Rowe Hospital, now an apartment building, served Wrangell until closing in 1968 when it was replaced by the present hospital. (Courtesy of MCN.)

The Wrangell Telephone Exchange housed the Wrangell Telephone Company from 1923 to 1962. It was operated by Christine Voss and, later, by her daughter Dorothy Voss Ottesen, pictured above. The building was located on Cow Alley and still stands, abandoned. Besides placing calls, the operator would also dispense boat news and the time of day. (Courtesy of Dorothy Ottesen.)

Cable was finally laid in 1906, enabling Wrangell to communicate with the outside world. In 1929, radio (wireless) brought improved communication to Seattle and to ships in northern waters. Messages could also be sent from the Wrangell Hotel and, later, from the post office. This building, the former wireless office, stands on the corner of Second and Fort Streets and is now a private home. (Photograph by Fred. D. Cheney; courtesy of the WM.)

This is the Rufus Sylvester house, still standing next to the post office. Sylvester built his fortune operating fur trading posts in the Alaska interior before moving to Wrangell in 1884. He bought a mercantile store and wharf before opening a sawmill with Thomas Willson in 1889. The house was originally one story and appears in many early photographs of the fort. (Courtesy of the WM.)

Sam Cunningham married Albertine Lemieux and bought this house prior to 1912. In 1919, he built a house next door, now owned by Olga Norris. Pictured are Albertine and children Beryl, Coralie, Fred, and Wilhelmina. In 1927, it became the Yellow Front Paint Store. The family sold it in 1957. For a time it was a house of ill repute, but today it is the Salvation Army thrift store. (Courtesy of Rose (Cunningham) Morgan.)

This garden was located on Cow Alley, so named because cows were driven down it after being banned from Front Street in 1910. The house pictured now belongs to the Urata family. It was built by 1914 and owned by John Grant, who also owned the telephone building next door. To the left is a corner of the Lemieux building that was located behind Angerman's store. (Courtesy of Bryant Benjamin.)

This strawberry patch on the corner of Second and Greif Streets was another flourishing garden. In the rear is the brick house built by Antime Lemieux. He also owned a large tract of land that he farmed behind the house. The bricks may have arrived as ballast on steamships. (Photograph by John E. Worden; courtesy of Leonard Campbell.)

This house, situated on the site of Sentry Hardware, was the home of Tlingit leader William Lewis, founder of the Thlingit Trading Company in 1907. Lewis bought this house in 1919 from the sawmill. He also owned a skating rink and movie house where, in 1934, the Alaska Native Brotherhood (ANB) hall was built using lumber from the dismantled Warde Cove cannery. (Courtesy of the WM.)

Lewis served as an Indian policeman, was elected to the town council, and was president of the Alaska Labor Union, a fishermen's organization. In 1924, he significantly remodeled his house, which has since been demolished to make way for Sentry Hardware. Lewis's daughter Tillie and son-in-law Elmer Carlstrom later owned the house, and Elmer took over management of the Thlingit Trading Company. (Courtesy of Dorothy Ottesen.)

The public school building became the town hall in 1931 after the school moved out. Prior to that time, the city council met in various locations, including upstairs in the Patenaude building. In 1911, Ole Johnson built the first town hall (today's largely unchanged senior center). The first library or reading room was also in that town hall. It moved in 1931 to the building seen here. Besides city offices, this building housed the mortuary, jail, doctor's office, an insurance business, and the museum and art center. It opened as a museum in 1967 under the direction of Lempi Fykerude. The Wrangell Civic Club was responsible for energetically and persistently generating support for the library and the museum, as well as for the playground next door. The building was also the first home of KSTK public radio. The bear totems eventually began to decay and are now in storage. Before the building was demolished in 1996, a group of former students gathered in front of their old school for one last picture. (Courtesy of the WM.)

The area of Wrangell north of the fort was originally called Foreign Town. In this section lived Alaska Natives from other tribes and those Stikine Tlingit who had married outside the tribe. The fort was surrounded by a stockade with gates on both the north and south offering the only access through the town. A boardwalk connecting this part of town with Front Street was built in 1918. In 1931, a road to Standard Oil (near today's Petroglyph Beach) was established and later extended to the Alaska Packers Association cannery (today's airport). Many residents of the north end had their own boathouses, some with rails to haul boats above the tide line, and docks. Photographs of this end of Wrangell are rare; this one dates from about 1911. Many of these homes are now gone, but the square hip-roofed Ferguson house is still standing. (Courtesy of MCN.)

Four

BOATS

Southeast Alaskans own more boats per capita than any place in the nation, and the reason why is not hard to fathom. With its uncounted islands and mountainous mainland, water is often the easiest mode of travel, as well as the source of a wealth of seafood and wildlife.

Long before there were streets and sidewalks in Wrangell, water was the roadway. Not only did it bring in paddle wheelers, steamships, and ferries, but also, from the earliest days, it was a means of local transportation. Tlingit canoes ranged in size from one-person hulls to Haida-crafted vessels 60 feet long. The Tlingit were more at home on water than on the land, not only on saltwater but, in the case of the Stikine Tlingit, on the roiling, silty waters of the Stikine River as well.

The gold rushes brought steamers from the cities of the south and paddle wheelers to navigate the shallow, but dangerous, Stikine River. These paddle wheelers were first wood-fired, later gas-powered, then diesel-powered. Besides providing Wrangell with all the necessities of life, the steamers also brought tourists. Several steamship lines made regular stops in Wrangell. There were also scheduled riverboat trips up the Stikine as far as Telegraph Creek. Wrangell served as a supply center for miners, big game hunters, and government workers headed for interior British Columbia.

Fishermen—trollers, gillnetters and seiners—all needed boats. At one time, over 400 boats were registered to Wrangell's commercial fishermen. The canneries used larger tenders and scows to pick up the catch from far-flung fishermen. During the early days, canneries employed sailing ships to transport the season's fish pack and workers to and from the canneries.

As Alaska began to export timber, log ships docked at Wrangell's wharfs to load timber bound for points south and to Asia.

Wrangell remains an island unconnected by bridges to the mainland. The Alaska Marine Highway is the well-named route to the rest of the world. Boats are not a luxury, but a necessity.

This boat is an example of a war canoe, although it was used for freighting and travel. The Haida Indians made and traded these large boats crafted from red cedar. A brown bear looking forward and another on the stern gave this canoe its name, Chief Shakes's *Brown Bear Canoe*. This photograph, taken near Shustak Point on the harbor's south shore, dates from about 1887 and shows several tourists sitting forward. (Courtesy of MCN.)

Chief Shakes owned two canoes. This is the smaller of the two, and besides family use, it was put into service ferrying visitors to and from Shakes Island. Tom Case Sr., Wrangell businessman, is seated second from the right and is identified in handwriting on the photograph. His wife, Emma, is holding a baby in this image captured around 1905. For several years, Shakes donated his canoes for Fourth of July boat races. (Courtesy of the WM.)

Riverboats varied in size and power. This Native-style canoe would have been poled and hauled upriver with lines. Later, many were powered with gas engines. The boat *Big Chief* was built by Farquahar Matheson in 1919 and was used to haul hunting parties, freight, and mail to Telegraph Creek. The trip took about 59 hours upriver and 13 down. (Photograph by Fred D. Cheney; courtesy of the WM.)

The *Telegraph* was launched in 1910 in Seattle. It carried passengers and cargo to Telegraph Creek, running up and back in five days. In 1912, it was remodeled with a gas engine and used for packing fish and cargo between Wrangell, Ideal Cove, and the fishing grounds. It is shown here at the floating dock around 1912. (Courtesy of the WM.)

Leo McCormack once recounted the history of the family's dock, seen here around 1900. William "King" Lear constructed the dock in 1875. In 1889, it was rebuilt for Rufus Sylvester and Robert Reid. Patrick C. McCormack, father of Leo, purchased the dock in 1907, renaming it the Saint Michael Trading Company Wharf and, later, the McCormack Dock Company. The Wrangell City Dock occupies the site today. (Courtesy of MCN.)

In this photograph is a steamship at the Canadian Pacific Railroad dock, built to the north of the McCormack Dock around 1898 or 1899. To the left is the steamship office, and on the right are totems in front of Matheson's and Walter Waters' Ivory Shop, which operated from the Matheson building for a few years beginning in 1928. The curio shop would have sold this as a postcard. (Courtesy of MCN.)

Tourists were attracted to Wrangell by its totems and Alaska Native dwellings. Here, visitors stand outside the Kadashan house, located on today's lower Front Street. By 1894, many Native families had abandoned their traditional houses for those of western design. The SS *Queen* of the Pacific Steamship Company is at dock. This iron ship, built in 1882, made round trips from Seattle to Southeast Alaska ports every two weeks with passengers, but also carried freight both north and south. The ship was commanded by Capt. James Carroll, who was rumored to engage in bootlegging during the course of the ship's travels. Regular ports of call were Ketchikan, Wrangell, Petersburg, Juneau, Sitka, and Skagway. In 1904, the *Queen* caught fire at the mouth of the Columbia River with a loss of 14 passengers. Behind the house to the rear is a building of the Willson and Sylvester Mill. Soon, the mill would surround and eventually engulf the house. (Courtesy of MCN.)

This photograph shows the SS *Princess Louise* approaching the Canadian Pacific Railroad dock in 1906. This ship first came to Wrangell during the Cassiar rush. It served canneries and logging camps and promoted Alaska with the Totem Pole Route. In 1936, this ship made a special trip to Southeast Alaska, bringing food to alleviate a shortage caused by a maritime strike. (Courtesy of the WM.)

The *Alki* was first brought to Alaska to use as a prison ship for captured whalers. In 1896 it entered the Alaska passenger trade and was nicknamed the "Stikine Flyer." She also hauled prospectors to the Yukon River. The *Alki* was lost during a blinding snowstorm off Point Augustus in Icy Strait in 1917. This photograph dates from about 1913. (Courtesy of the WM.)

This image of the *Star of Bengal* was captured just months before it was wrecked on Coronation Island on September 20, 1908. The ship was one of the Alaska Packers Association's star fleet. These ships were used to transport workers, mostly Chinese, north, and carry the year's salmon pack south to San Francisco. In what was at the time considered a disaster without parallel in the history of the Alaska salmon industry, the ship left the Wrangell cannery at Point Highfield under tow by two small cannery tugboats and headed for the open sea. A storm came up during the night as they neared Coronation Island. After fighting unsuccessfully to pull away from the rocky coast, the tugs cut their lines and the *Star of Bengal* foundered on the island's south shore with 110 out of 137 lives lost. In 1928, the last ship of the star fleet left Wrangell. Youngsters Leonard Campbell and Julius Mason were aboard the tug that towed that ship to sea. (Photograph by John E. Worden; courtesy of the WM.)

Sails were used on canoes to help ascend the Stikine before engines came into use. Native sails are said to have been made of woven cedar bark and later, of cotton, although according to anthropologist George Emmons, the Tlingit had no history of using sails before contact with white traders and explorers. These canoes lacked a keel and center or sideboards and sailed only with the wind. (Courtesy of the WM.)

Telegraph Creek was the terminus for traffic to the interior. Beginning with the Stikine rush in 1862, a wide variety of boats made the 150-mile trip from Wrangell. Following the Klondike rush, Telegraph Creek became the business and administrative center of Northern British Columbia. Pack trails led inland to the Cassiar mining district. The village is pictured here with an unidentified paddle wheeler. (Photograph by John E. Worden; courtesy of the WM.)

Owned by the Hudson's Bay Company, the *Port Simpson* made several trips to Glenora or Telegraph Creek each season until 1916. She was called "the best appointed sternwheeler on the Pacific Coast." The *Port Simpson* carried passengers and freight and also offered day excursions from Wrangell to Great Glacier "for those who wished to get off on the ice" at a fare of $1.50. (Courtesy of the WM.)

Three boats bore the name *Hazel B No. 3*, all owned by the Barrington brothers Sid, Hill, and Harry, and named after Sid's wife. The first was built in 1916. Pictured here is the third, built in 1926, which plied the river until 1946. It had 22 staterooms and could carry 50 passengers and 40 tons of freight. Boats left Wrangell every 48 hours. (Courtesy of the WM.)

When the long-anticipated New York–to–Nome planes arrived on Sergief Island on August 14, 1920, most of Wrangell boarded the Hazel B Nos. 3 and 4 to witness the landing. Shown are the boats and barge leaving after the planes landed. The man with the camera is Wrangell photographer Richard Suratt, who was on hand to take pictures for the Fox News Agency. (Courtesy of the WM.)

The mail boat Princess Pat was owned by Walter Waters. He carried mail, freight, and passengers between Wrangell and the West Coast of Prince of Wales Island. Mail was brought to Wrangell by steamer and then distributed to villages, camps, canneries, and the Cassiar. Starting in 1887 the Iris, and later the Baranof, which was owned by Leonard M. Churchill and William Taylor, delivered the mail. (Courtesy of MCN.)

The USS *Patterson* was a US Coast Guard and Geodetic Survey (later the United States Geodetic Survey or USGS) ship that operated in Alaska, taking soundings in the region's mostly uncharted waters. The USGS began surveying with wire drags in 1915 in order to locate reefs and pinnacles too often discovered by tragic accident. This photograph dates from 1916. The USGS maintained warehouses in Wrangell. (Photograph by John E. Worden; courtesy of MCN.)

This image illustrates the variety of vessels that could be found tied up in Wrangell harbor during the town's fishing heyday. Although labeled "power fishing boats," seine boat and gillnetters powered by muscle are also in evidence. In 1929, more than 200 gas boats were counted in Wrangell's mosquito fleet. (Courtesy of MCN.)

This photograph of Wrangell harbor taken from Shustak Point dates from between 1926 and 1930. The harbor breakwater was constructed in 1925 and the float in 1926. Tied at the dock are two Barrington riverboats as well as several launches and a hand troller. Prior to construction of the breakwater that added much-needed secure anchorage for Wrangell boats, sternwheelers were brought ashore in the Inner Harbor or on Shustak Point for the winter. A seine boat is

approaching the float on the right. Features of the town, from the left, include the McCormack Dock with a steamer, the original Presbyterian Church before the fire in 1930, the sawmill dock, the Wrangell Packing Company building on that dock, and piles of sawn lumber stacked along the waterfront. Also constructed in 1926 was the Bishop Rowe Hospital, visible on the hillside at right rear. (Courtesy of Leonard and Lynne Campbell.)

Hansen's Boat Shop was started by brothers Olaf and Alf Hansen. The large building was constructed in 1916. On the left is the salmon tender *Afognak*. The *Nebraska* on the right was last used as a troller by Ed and Norma Loftus but had been previously captained by Charles Moore and owned by the Wrangell Packing Company. This photograph dates from the 1940s. (Courtesy of the WM.)

Pictured here in 1945 is a Grumman Goose plane similar to those used by Ellis Air and Alaska Coastal Air. The fondly remembered Goose could land on both water and shore. Wrangell got its first airmail in 1923 when the seaplane *Northland* arrived from Lake Bay. Wrangell's first hydroplane airport was constructed south of the cemetery in 1930. Its pilings are still visible. (Courtesy of the WM.)

Five

MAKING A LIVING ON LAND AND SEA

The Tlingit had always been experts at living off the land and sea. With the arrival of white men, fishing, hunting, and trapping continued and were used to acquire cash. Furs attracted traders who came to Southeast Alaska in the late 18th century. Trapping and fur farming continued to be a seasonal source of income for both Alaska Natives and white men well into the 20th century.

Salmon canneries and salteries sprang up in the late 19th century as declining salmon stocks in the lower 48 states led to increased attention to Alaska's untouched resource. In the 1920s, shrimp and crab fisheries and processors, as well as cold storage companies, were also established in Wrangell. To man the canneries, Chinese workers from San Francisco and other cities were brought to Wrangell. Resident Natives and whites also worked on the cannery lines. Fish traps efficiently harvested salmon. These traps, owned by absentee corporations and independent operators, had a negative effect on salmon populations. The traps became a bitter issue among residents of the territory and were eventually a factor in the push for statehood. From the beginning, Wrangell was and still is home base for a considerable fleet of fishermen.

The Willson and Sylvester Mill Company was launched in 1889, first to support the canneries' requirements and, later, to supply milled lumber for Wrangell's increasing building needs. Independent loggers harvested timber along the shoreline using hand tools and, later, steam donkeys. Mechanization increased over the years in the woods and also in the mills. The Wrangell Mill entered the international market in the 1950s with its acquisition by a Japanese company.

Wrangell was also the supply and transport center for mining operations in the Cassiar District of British Columbia. Locally, claims were filed in Groundhog Basin, the Virginia Lake area, and on Zarembo Island. Marble quarries, such as those at Tokeen and Blake (Ham) Island, and garnet mining all created interest and occasional profit for local prospectors.

Agriculture on a small scale was attempted on Farm (earlier known as Brown's) Island, and over the years, several dairies operated in and around the town.

The Alaska Packer's Association (APA) cannery at Point Highfield is pictured here in 1911. This plant was built by the Glacier Packing Company, but it joined the powerful APA, the largest salmon packer in Alaska, in 1893. Each of the company's canneries was identified as a diamond followed by an initial. Thus, Wrangell was the Diamond W. It operated until 1927 and was dismantled in 1930. Prior to the use of gas engines, oars powered both troll and net fishers. Roofed scows, as seen here, were towed to popular trolling places to take on the catch. Small launches, such as those anchored here, were sent to tend four-oared seine boats on distant fishing grounds. At the wharf is one of the APA's star fleet ships, probably the *Star of Greenland*. These slow iron-hulled boats were outpaced by steam but suited the seasonal salmon trade and were cheap. At the time of this photograph, there was no road from town, although there was a footpath. (Photograph by John E. Worden; courtesy of MCN.)

The *Star of Greenland* was an iron-hulled ship built in 1892 for the clipper trade. It was originally named the *Hawaiian Isles* and was purchased and renamed by the APA in 1910. It sailed in a number of capacities and under several names until it was scrapped in 1957. The *Star of Greenland* was Wrangell's station ship from 1914 to 1920 and again in 1922. (Photograph by John E. Worden; courtesy of the WM.)

Early Alaska canneries contracted with brokers to bring in gangs of Chinese workers to handle all phases of salmon canning from manufacturing cans to loading ships. In 1904, mechanization began to replace some hand labor. The Iron Chink eliminated many workers who had butchered, cleaned, and trimmed each fish. Shown here is the interior of the APA cannery in 1914. (Photograph by John E. Worden; courtesy of the WM.)

Before 1899, only a few schooners fished for halibut, and halibut banks were unknown. The fish were caught from dories with long lines and bottom trawls. Pictured are workers in 1911 at the Columbia and Northern Fishing and Packing Company, whose wharf and plant were located near Lynch Street. Catches were frozen in glacier ice, earning fishermen 5½¢ a pound. (Photograph by R. Livesay; courtesy of the WM.)

In the center front is a small gillnetter. The gas boat behind would have towed the dory to the fishing grounds and served as living quarters. These independent fishermen gradually monopolized the Stikine River fisheries unsuitable for larger boats. Salmon prices at the time of this photograph, around 1907, were 2½¢ per sockeye. The *Wrangell Sentinel* reported in 1903 that 400 men were fishing with nets. (Courtesy of Leonard and Lynne Campbell.)

Around 1885, a Norwegian fisherman demonstrated to a few Alaskans how to drag hooks baited with herring to catch salmon. It wasn't until 1910, however, that a commercial salmon trolling fleet became established. Rowboats with sails were used, and around 1915, powerboats began to come into use. The previous year, the Alaska Trollers Protective Association was organized to sell salmon packed in ice to Seattle markets. These two photographs show trollers at two of Wrangell's favorite fishing grounds. In 1924, Wrangellite Steve Shepard invented an improved gurdy (a spool with crank to haul in fishing lines) and planned to manufacture it at the Wrangell Machine Shop (the site of City Market today). The first shrimp fishery in town opened nearby in the Wrangell Narrows in 1915 and crab began to be harvested and canned in 1920. (Above, courtesy of the WM; below, courtesy of MCN.)

The Sanitary Packing Company, built in 1912 and seen here in about 1915, was located on the site of the ferry terminal. It burned in 1924. There were floating crab, shrimp, and salmon canneries anchored in front of Shakes Island and in the Inner Harbor at this time and through the 1920s. In 1933, Karl Thiele built the Diamond K salmon cannery on this site. (Courtesy of MCN.)

The McCormack Dock is shown in this image from the 1920s. The Wrangell Shellfish Company opened in 1923 to can shrimp, and in 1925, George and Joe Sumption established Reliance Shrimp. The Wrangell Cold Storage and Ice Company also built a plant (center) in 1924. For most of the decade, shrimp fishing and processing was the only winter payroll. (Courtesy of the WM.)

These are the seiners *Grace, Nebraska*, and an unidentified boat tied up at the Wrangell Packing Company dock in 1937. The processor was organized in 1929 and located on the sawmill dock. The man on the right is owner Frank S. Barnes, who was killed by a brown bear on the Stikine in 1940. His wife, Doris, later became mayor, territorial representative, and senator. (Courtesy of the WM.)

The Diamond K Packing Company, typical of many canneries, reorganized a number of times. In 1947, fire destroyed the cannery, which was then named the Far West Wrangell Company. The cannery ship *Admiral Rogers* was at the wharf and helped fight the fire, saving neighboring houses. Two years later, Harbor Seafoods, today's Trident Seafoods, opened a new cannery on the downtown waterfront. (Courtesy of the WM.)

Charles Benjamin and Albert Carlstrom worked as hand loggers, as seen in this photograph from about 1909. Benjamin earned money logging to purchase his mercantile store. The men are cutting with a two-man saw and standing on springboards used to elevate them above the spreading butt of the tree. (Courtesy of Bryant Benjamin.)

The steam donkey was a winch that became popular around 1880. It consisted of a boiler and an engine mounted on a sled. Early logging had to be done near water. The donkey was used to skid or drag logs from hillsides to the shore. They were then rafted and hauled to the sawmill. This photograph of a floating steam donkey dates from about 1915. (Courtesy of the WM.)

The Wrangell Shingle Company, located on Case Avenue, was started in 1907 by J.W. Gano and was able to produce 40,000 shingles a day. Fritz Angerman purchased it in 1931. In 1941, the Wrangell Lumber Mill built a new shingle mill that continued to operate as Wrangell Cedar Products after World War II. This is operator Frank Smith in about 1911. (Courtesy of the WM.)

In 1900, Tlingit landowners John Kadashan and George Shakes sold property to the sawmill for its expansion. It grew to surround the Kadashan house, seen in this photograph with an unidentified man. The mill used to pile slabs on its dock, but one day it collapsed and lumber floated everywhere. Perhaps that is the story behind the lumber covering the beach in this photograph. (Courtesy of MCN.)

The lumber industry began as a support for mining and commercial fishing. Sawmills supplied canneries with wooden shipping boxes for cans and lumber for fish traps, warehouses, barracks, and houses. Thomas A. Willson and Rufus Sylvester established Wrangell's first mill, the Willson and Sylvester Mill Company, in 1889, and by the next year, it was considered the largest in the territory. After both Willson and Sylvester died, Harry Gartley, Sylvester's son-in-law, organized a new company called Willson and Sylvester Incorporated. The mill burned in 1918 but was rebuilt the next year. Beginning in 1926, the mill also produced electric power for the community and the company name was changed to Wrangell Lumber and Power Company. In 1926, the company added a deepwater dock and entered the export business, sending lumber to the United Kingdom. Replacement of wooden salmon boxes with cardboard in the 1930s hurt the company, which up until that time had employed about 100 mill hands. The mill changed ownership and names, and during World War II, it was shut down in disrepair. (Photograph by John E. Worden; courtesy of the WM.)

C.T. Takahashi of Seattle bought the mill in 1949 for $35,000. In 1954, the Japanese-owned Alaska Lumber and Pulp Company leased the Wrangell Lumber Company and began exporting to Japan in the next year. In 1981, the rundown plant, now the reorganized Alaska Wood Products, was shut down and a new facility was built at 6-Mile. This photograph dates from around the 1930s. (Courtesy of the WM.)

Wrangell had small dairies from the days of the Presbyterian mission farm on Farm Island. This photograph from the 1950s shows cows from Nore's Dairy ambling along the shore of Sergief Island. The cattle were barged to the island in the Stikine River delta each spring to forage for the summer. A skiff brought milk to town every day. (Courtesy of MCN.)

The Russians began trading with the Aleuts for sea otter, and by the second half of the 18th century, they had nearly depleted that animal. They also traded for mink, marten, beaver, sea otter, and other furs. All traders found the Alaska Natives to be excellent negotiators. During the Stikine Gold Rush, Natives hauled freight, enabling them to earn cash for traps and guns. The photograph above shows two hunters, probably Tahltan Indians, with their take from 1920. Bear hunters in the early 20th century image below display their spring bear catch and mountain goat pelts. Hunting and trapping provided seasonal work for many in Wrangell. In the 1920s, four fur buyers advertised each week in the *Wrangell Sentinel*. (Above, photograph by John E. Worden, courtesy of the WM; below, photograph by Fred D. Cheney, courtesy of MCN.)

Fox farming grew rapidly in Southeast Alaska during the 1920s. Soon, there were fox and mink farms on islands near Wrangell. An island could be leased from the US Forest Service for $25 a year and canneries provided cheap feed. Other farmers such as the Nore family seen here in 1953—Ingvald with nephews Michael, Charlie, Tom, and Bob—raised mink in the building behind them on Wrangell Island. (Courtesy of MCN.)

The Alaska Garnet Mining and Manufacturing Company, possibly the first all-woman corporation in the United States, was organized in 1906 to develop a mine at Garnet Ledge near the mouth of the Stikine River. This may be one of the owners with a handful of the garnets near the mine in 1911. The mine today is deeded to the Presbyterian Church for the use of local children who sell garnets to tourists. (Photograph by Fed Cheney; courtesy of the WM.)

Marble was discovered on Marble Island on the west coast of Prince of Wales Island in 1899. It was worked by the Vermont Marble Company, which also did work on Ham Island, until 1926. Blocks were lifted by derrick and dragged to a wharf by rail and sledge. In 1915, the date of the image above, the mine employed about 60 men who lived in the small community of Tokeen. (Courtesy of MCN.)

The Cassiar District of British Columbia experienced several 20th-century gold rushes beginning in 1913. A road constructed between Telegraph Creek and Dease Lake for the Gold Pan Rush of 1925 made vehicle travel to mining claims a possibility for the first time. Shown here that year are miners, packhorses, and trucks preparing to head to Telegraph Creek aboard the *Hazel B* boats and barges. (Courtesy of MCN.)

Six

THE FOURTH OF JULY

Among the major holidays of the year, the Fourth of July ranks high in Wrangell as a time of enthusiastic patriotism mixed with the joy of homecoming and the excitement of contests. The day was celebrated in 1898 with a literal bang with a 45-gun salute shot off at noon. The noisemaker, a gift from the Russians, was a cannon that belonged to Kadashan. Fireworks were a part of the celebration from the earliest years, although fear of flames following the disastrous 1906 fire prompted a warning in the newspaper to shoot them off only near the water. Worries about enemy sabotage prompted a ban on fireworks for the 1942 celebration.

In 1905, the *Alaska Sentinel* announced what was a typical outline of the day: a patriotic program in the morning that included singing led by the children, a recitation of the Declaration of Independence, and an oration by the Rev. Henry P. Corser. The afternoon, in a tradition carried into the present, was devoted to street games. The games have changed some over the years. A hundred years ago, the races included foot races for boys, girls, and old men, a pie-eating contest for boys, a shoe-tying contest, and boxing. Water sports competitions in swimming and log rolling followed, culminating with boat races for canoes and gas launches. A few years later, the day was expanded as invitations were sent out to Shakan, Klawock, Santa Ana, and Petersburg. Shakan and Klawock arrived with brass bands aboard a barge. The first parade, led by the Kake band, was held in 1911.

Businesses and citizens donated money for prizes and the fireworks displays in early days. Beginning in 1950, the Fourth of July queen contest raised funds, a tradition that endures along with the original celebratory spirit.

The photograph above, probably taken from the balcony of Bruno Greif's Brewery, later called the Norris building, shows Front Street decorated with bunting. The crowd appears to be gathering to hear the traditional Fourth of July oration, to be followed by races of various sorts. The scene predates the 1906 fire. Below is the men's race during the holiday in the early 1900s. Races in 1918 included a Fat Man's Race. The Fat Ladies Race failed to materialize due to lack of entrants. In many years, there was also a parade led by visiting Alaska Native bands. (Above, courtesy of WM; below, courtesy of Bryant Benjamin.)

Street races were an important feature of Wrangell's Fourth of July, as they remain today. Depending on the year, there were foot races for girls and boys, bicycle races, greased pig races for men, boys, and ladies, a rifle shoot, and, often, a boxing match. These photographs depicting the girls' and boys' races date from about 1915 and show the north end of Front Street. There were money prizes for the races that were donated by local business and individuals. In 1918, prizes were awarded in Thrift and War Savings Stamps to help support the war effort. The queen contest, which raises contest prize money today, began in 1950. Queen Patricia Lewis and princesses Helen Angerman and Henrietta Bradley sold $2,000 worth of tickets that year. (Courtesy of the WM.)

The pie-eating contest was popular not only with boys but with onlookers as well, as seen in this image from about 1915. First place was a prize of $1.50. Some years featured cracker or watermelon-eating competitions instead. The egg toss and potato races were also included in some years' events, but in 1942, both were omitted due to a scarcity of food during World War II. (Courtesy of the WM.)

The three-legged race is underway in this photograph from 1929. The second racer from the left is Martin Nore. That year, the parade was led by nurses and included a boys' band, the Alaska Native Brotherhood and Sisterhood, and a Native band. Jim Nolan, owner of the Den O' Sweets (pictured on the right in front of the fire hall tower), sang popular songs at the dance that night. (Photograph by Battau; courtesy of MCN.)

Baseball games were also a part of Fourth of July celebrations. The first game held in the town's Recreation Park was played in 1915. Seen here that year, Wrangell played the Lake Bay cannery from Prince of Wales Island and won 6–3 before playing a second game against the Metlakatla Band team. Rufus Sylvester pitched his first game that day. (Courtesy of Bryant Benjamin.)

Wrangell's first float was paraded in 1911. The float seen here dates from 1920. The next year, another float featured Ruth Sylvester as the Goddess of Liberty, Helen Fletcher as Justice, and young Valentine Gartley as Uncle Sam. This float is parked in front of the public school, which is now the site of a park and library. (Courtesy of MCN.)

Boat races were a favorite feature of Wrangell's Fourth. Rowboats and canoes competed in early races, with Chief Shakes lending two war canoes in 1922. There were also gas launch races each year to 5-Mile Island and back. Pictured here are such launches in 1909. Races were held for three categories of engine, 15- through 80-horsepower. There was not an event for outboard motors until 1927. The next year, Wrangell Motors advertised outboard motors for sale for "thrill-seekers." In later years, races between massive tugboats were a highlight. Due to the Depression, only rowboat races were held during 1931. The boats in the photograph, from sculls to Tlingit canoes to elegant launches, are tied to the floating dock near the McCormack Dock. In the background is the Willson and Sylvester sawmill. (Photograph by John E. Worden; courtesy of MCN.)

Seven

TOTEMS

Totem poles have been one of Wrangell's distinctive elements since the town's earliest days. Wealth from the fur trade, the introduction of steel tools, and individual artistry combined to generate a profusion of carven images that still enrich the town. The most prominent early carver, Kadjusdu. axtc II, crafted the Shakes House posts that, 300 years later, are the earliest posts known to exist. He was possibly the teacher of another fine carver known only as the "Fort Wrangell Master." The latter and Yiika.aas, or William Ukas, were responsible for half of the 23 totems standing in Wrangell prior to 1900. William's son Tom followed as another notable Wrangell carver.

The carving of totems by the Tlingit was probably adopted from the Haida and Tsimshian. Before the introduction of steel blades, poles were less elaborate, but new tools and prosperity produced a flowering of artistry and complexity in the 19th century prior to the devastating mid-century epidemics.

Early tourists were fascinated with the poles that lined the waterfront. The forest of poles reported in 1883, however, was reduced to only a handful a decade later. Missionaries, too, were attracted by the poles but often misinterpreted their meaning and function. By 1920, many original poles were beginning to deteriorate and the Alaska Native community offered to give them to the town if a park could be set aside for them. That was not to happen for many more years. Still, Wrangell's leaders recognized the attraction of totems to visitors. The Rev. Henry P. Corser helped make the oral histories behind the poles accessible to non-Native readers. New copies of poles and originals were carved for the dedication of the restored Chief Shakes Tribal House in 1940. Reflecting a resurgence of interest in the carving tradition, Steve Brown, Will Burkhart II, and Wayne Price carved poles for Front Street's Totem Park in the 1980s. Interest and care for totems continues today as funds are sought to duplicate existing deteriorating poles and create new ones to reflect and honor Wrangell's heritage.

These killer whales mark the gravesite of Kow-ish-te, or Chief Shakes V, on Case Avenue. The killer whales, seen here about 1915, are the second of three that have distinguished the site. Shakes died in 1878 after living through a time of great change. The Emancipation Proclamation that freed American slaves also liberated Tlingit slaves. This loss of property eroded the power of the Tlingit upper class. (Photograph by Henry P. Corser; courtesy of MCN.)

The Kit totem is seen here around 1887 standing on Shustak Point. This pole is attributed to the Fort Wrangell Master. Steve Brown, Wayne Burkhart, and Wayne Price re-carved the pole, and it was erected in Totem Park in 1987. The symbol of a kit, or killer whale, is prized because it is a strong, brave creature and able to kill whales. (Photograph by William or Edward Partridge; courtesy of MCN.)

The two poles at the front of the Shakes House are reported to have been carved in 1832. The stereoscope photograph above dates from about 1870. The left pole is called the Double Finned Killer Whale Crest Hat or the Gonakadet pole. Both poles are mortuary poles and contained cremated ashes. The man in the cedar hat on the right may be Shakes V. (Courtesy of MCN.)

This photograph from around 1915 shows Gush-klin, also called Shakes VI, with one of his granddaughters. They stand in front of the Bear Up the Mountain pole. It was carved to replace one left at Old Town and is attributed to the Fort Wrangell Master. Civilian Conservation Corps carvers duplicated the totems in the late 1930s, and they were carved once more in 1984, making them the fourth generation. (Courtesy of MCN.)

This pole is one of many that were displaced as Wrangell grew. It was situated on today's Alaska Marine Lines property. The rear of the Sun House is visible to the left. The pole appears in photographs after 1868 and, according to carver Steve Brown, was the first multi-figure pole raised in Wrangell after the move from Old Town. This pole is attributed, again, to the Fort Wrangell Master. There are no remnants today. (Courtesy of MCN.)

Pictured is the Dogfish memorial pole, a burial monument now in storage in the National Museum of the American Indian near Washington, DC. It is possibly the last pole carved by Yiika.aas or William Ukas, who was aided by his son Tom. It stood on Cemetery Point until 1982. This picture dates from about 1898. (Photograph by Otto D. Goetze; courtesy of MCN.)

The Kiks.adi totem has been one of the most photographed in Wrangell since it was raised in 1894. Also known as the Kahl-teen pole, it was carved by William Ukas and memorializes the Kiks.adi leader Kahl-teen and his family, as well as the Shadesty family. The Kiks.adi name is derived from Kicks Bay, where they first stopped on their migration from the Nass River to the Stikine. The distinctive symbol on top represents the mountain on the Stikine River where the Kiks.adi camped during the flood. The frog is also a family crest symbol. The totem stands in front of the Kiks.adi family's Sun House on today's Totem Park in this photograph from about 1915. The house is named for a nephew's dream that a house with a round opening would bring good luck. Behind the Sun House is St. Philip's Gymnasium. This pole was re-carved by Brown, Burkhart, and Price and raised in Kiks.adi Totem Park in 1987. The original remains are in storage in Wrangell. (Photograph by LHP; courtesy of MCN.)

The Kadashan poles stand in front of the Kadashan house, located where the Marine Repair Facility is today. The original poles may have been erected soon after the Russian occupation of Wrangell. John Kadashan's brother erected the pole on the right, called the Lqiana'ki pole. According to Henry P. Corser, it is the older. Creator is carved in human form. In later poles, Raven is the creator. The left-hand pole is the Eagle pole, modeled on a Haida cane given to Kadashan. Eagle is the crest of the Kadashan family. In the 1920s, the Kadashan house, then surrounded by the sawmill, was torn down. However, in 1926, the Commercial Club realized the tourist potential of Wrangell's totems and paid to have Chilkat carver Tacook restore these poles. They were moved to the site of Alaska Marine Lines. Later, when they were beyond repair, the poles were duplicated and placed on Shakes Island, where they stand today. (Courtesy of MCN.)

The restored Kadashan totems stand at their second home on the corner of Front and Episcopal Streets in this photograph from the 1930s. The restoration was part of a growing appreciation in Southeast Alaska of the importance and transitory nature of totem poles. St. Philip's Episcopal Church can be seen in the background. (Photograph by Otto C. Schallerer; courtesy of the WM.)

This Flying Raven mortuary pole stood in the Alaska Native cemetery on Cemetery Point. Raven is carved demonstrating his dual personality—head and wings of a raven with a human-like body. It was carved by William Ukas and remained in place until it deteriorated. Note the One-Legged Fisherman pole in the right rear. A few headstones and fragments of fences survive in the cemetery today. (Courtesy of the WM.)

The Beaver pole stands in front of the Flying Raven House. The pole began as a grave marker on Shustak Point with only the beaver figure. By the 1890s, it had been moved to this location near today's Raime's Bar. The bottom portion was added telling the story of Duk'tool, or the "Strong Man," who tears a sea lion in half and is illustrated by the third figure from the top. The pole, except for the beaver, was sold in the 1940s to the Alaska State Museum. The house and pole appear again in the photograph below taken about 1900. Here, tourists negotiate the precarious boardwalks of the early village. In the background left is Chief Shakes V's gravesite, and in the back right is the Shakes House and Raven pole. (Left, photograph by John E. Worden; below, photograph by William H. Rau; both courtesy of MCN.)

The Kit and Wolf totems were grave totems, sitting atop grave houses, some of which were located near homes on lower Front Street. The log grave house in the 1880s pictured above shows Russian influence with rounded timbers. Before their arrival, the Tlingit often squared their logs with adzes. Traditionally, Tlingit grave houses were near and often behind the clan house. In Wrangell, the area between Front and Church Streets served as a burial ground. In the 1900 photograph below, the Kit totem appears on the fort grounds. The Wolf totem was also moved and appears in later images in front of the Kadashan house on the ground beside the two Kadashan totems. (Above, photograph by Truman W. Ingersoll; courtesy of MCN.)

The Raven totem was carved by William Ukas in 1896 and raised by Shakes VI. The original stood in front of the Shakes family home on Church Street, the site of the Bible Baptist Church today. The Shakes family eventually moved here, and the clan house on Shakes Island was opened as a tourist attraction. The pole fell and broke into pieces in a 1982 windstorm. Tom Ukas carved a smaller copy that stands in front of the post office. A full-sized version has been re-carved by Steve Brown, Will Burkhart II, and Wayne Price and stands in Kiks.adi Totem Park. The pole retells the familiar story of Raven bringing daylight to the world. The remains of the Raven pole are in storage in Wrangell. (Photograph by John E. Worden; courtesy of MCN.)

The Witchcraft totem, carved in Haida style, stood at the entrance to the McCormack Dock. It depicts the story of a young girl left to starve who was told by an oystercatcher, at top, where to find magic boxes giving her shamanic powers. The totem was brought from the deserted village of Howkan on Prince of Wales Island in 1922. Haida villages on Prince of Wales Island were abandoned in 1911 when the government wanted them to consolidate schools. The Haida people moved to Hydaburg while Tlingit villagers resettled in Klawock. Below, the Gunyah totem stood next to the Matheson store. Matheson bought a group of poles from an abandoned West Coast village. At the time this photograph was taken in the 1920s, the board street leading to Cow Alley was named Totem Street and considered the shortest street in town. (Right, courtesy of the WM; below, courtesy of MCN.)

The One-legged Fisherman pole stood on Cemetery Point and relates the story of Kayak, a mythological Tlingit hero. Shakes VII had the pole carved in 1898 by William Ukas in memory of his uncle Kaukish who had died the previous year. A replica raised in 1987 and carved by Steve Brown, Will Burkhart, and Wayne Prices stands in the Kiks.adi Totem Park. The replica is based on a similar pole photographed at Old Town in 1910 and sketched by John Muir in 1879. In the photograph below, the One-legged Fisherman is already beginning to age. Grave fences and a grave house surround it. Fragments of the original pole are on display at the Wrangell Museum, and the rest is in storage. (Left, courtesy of MCN; below, photograph by Fred D. Cheney; courtesy of the WM.)

Pictured is the last remaining building of Fort Wrangell. It was a one-story, whitewashed log building that served as the quartermaster's storehouse and local health center, among other purposes, but was finally used as a meeting place, or dugout, for the American Legion. In 1941, it was moved on rollers to a site beside today's public library. Johnny James carved the two totems that belong to the Katcadi or Tiinedi clan in the late 1930s. The pole on the left recalls the story of a boy captured by Dog Salmon. His wolf father holds him. The story of two men who killed Octopus is related on the right hand pole. The poles stood until 1993 when they were removed during the library's renovation. They now stand in the Nolan Civic Center lobby along with plaques relating their stories. (Courtesy of the WM.)

On June 3, 1940, a new totem, the tallest in Alaska for a time, was raised on Front Street near the entrance to the Canadian Steamship dock. Its carving and raising were a part of the celebration of Wrangell's Tlingit heritage during the Chief Shakes House restoration. The pole was carved by the Chilkat carver Tacook of Haines, called at the time "the last of the great Indian carvers." Wrangell businessmen Leo McCormack and Walter Waters commissioned the pole. After the 1952 fire, the totem sat unattended for years. McCormack and Mable Waters sold the pole to the city for $1 in 1964, and in 1974, it was refurbished and erected on the city hall lawn until it began to show signs of rot. It is in storage today. The pole tells three stories: *How Raven Got Daylight*, *Jonah and the Cannibal Giant*, and *Mosquito*. (Photograph by Mary Allen; courtesy of MCN.)

Eight
PEOPLE

Wrangell has been a melting pot from its earliest days. Prior to settlement by Russians, the Stikine Tlingit had numerous villages in the area. With the influx of first Russian, then British traders, clans began to move nearby to take advantage of fur trading opportunities. Besides the Stikine Tlingit, Alaska Natives from other tribes moved here and settled north of the fort in Foreign Town. Contact with whites soon proved detrimental as disease and alcohol took their toll. When Presbyterian missionaries arrived in 1876, they began to educate the Native people, as well as attempt to curb some abuses. While they made great strides in assimilating Natives into modern life, they were also responsible for fostering a decline in Tlingit culture and language. In the 20th century, however, two Wrangell Tlingits, Charlie Jones and Tillie Paul Tamaree, spearheaded a fight to obtain the vote for Alaska Natives. The building of the Chief Shakes Tribal House signaled the beginning of a resurgence of Tlingit culture that is ongoing today.

The discovery of gold in 1862, 1873, and again in 1898 brought hopeful white men and women to Wrangell. Some, disappointed in their search for riches, stayed to found a community. As the Cassiar rush dwindled, Chinese miners worked old claims and were also added to Wrangell's mix. Contrary to earlier booms, Wrangell's population did not plunge following the Klondike rush. Fledgling lumber and fishing industries drew those interested in beginning a new life in the North. These included arrivals from all parts of Europe and North America. Wrangell became a hub for business and industry in the region, including Telegraph Creek and the British Columbia interior.

Women were scarce during the gold rush era; however, as the town settled, bachelors married and married men sent for their families. Some families today can count four or more generations in Wrangell. Long-term timber sales in the 1950s caused Wrangell's population to rise, while the closure of the sawmill in the 1990s reversed the trend. Still, Wrangell remains a sturdy community with a colorful history woven from the lives of people from many lands and cultures.

Perhaps the first images of Wrangell were captured by photographer Edweard Muybridge. He visited Wrangell in 1868 with Maj. Gen. Henry Halleck. Halleck was inspecting Alaska for the new Military Department of Alaska. This Tlingit group is posed near what is today's lower Front Street. (See photographs on page 17 for comparison.) (Photograph by Edweard Muybridge; courtesy of MCN.)

This family group is posed next to a beautifully adze-smoothed canoe. This photograph was marketed to tourists in the 1880s. One of the first organized tours in Alaska took place in the summer of 1878 when Captain George S. Wright escorted a group up the Stikine River from Fort Wrangel. (Photograph by Goldsmith Brothers; courtesy of MCN.)

Matilda probably was a graduate of Amanda McFarland's mission school for girls. McFarland educated and taught Tlingit girls, particularly those without families, to run a Western-style household. Some of the most promising students were sent to the Indian School in Forest Grove and, later, to Chemawa, both in Oregon. This photograph dates from about 1887. (Photograph by Edward or William Partridge; courtesy of MCN.)

Three women pose in their regalia. From left to right, they are Mrs. Barney Williams; Susie Jones, wife of Kudanake (also called Charlie Jones or Shakes VII); and Tahltan Jennie. Jennie died in 1921, and her obituary in the *Wrangell Sentinel* included a poem in memory of her long marriage to noted hunter Tahltan Billy. Susie Jones is the daughter of Tahltan Jennie. (Photograph by John E. Worden; courtesy of the WM.)

At left is Chief Kadashan's clan house, built in traditional style of heavy spruce or red cedar planks. It appears to be under construction. Kadashan was considered a master of protocol and served as a peacemaker, several times helping to prevent interclan warfare. Seen below in 1887, Kadashan built this much-photographed house, the first Western-style home in Wrangell, after seeing similar houses on a trip to Victoria, BC. Kadashan accompanied John Muir on his travels up the Stikine and around Southeast Alaska during 1879 and 1890. He also traveled with S. Hall Young as a diplomat and translator. The stories he told the Rev. Henry P. Corser make up most of the book *Totem Tales*. When the house was demolished in 1926, the poles were moved and restored by Tacook. (Photographs by Fred W. Cheney; courtesy of the WM.)

Chief Shakes Island is crowded with buildings in this photograph from around 1915. According to Tlingit historian Herb Bradley, the Tlingit used the island prior to Russian settlement when the Nan ya ayi people moved there. During the 1800s, four ancient house posts were brought from Old Town. On the left are Shustak Point and the Shustak houses. Logs for the sawmill are stored to the right of the island. Below, Shakes VI and two women sit inside the tribal house with a casket. They are surrounded by blankets with the clan's dogfish, killer whale, and bear symbols in this photograph from 1887. Shakes VI was chosen clan chief as a young man. A cast iron woodstove and chimney take the place of an earlier open fire pit. (Below, photograph by Edward or William Partridge; courtesy of MCN.)

During his tenure as chief, Shakes VI saw Tlingit culture weaken under the influence of missionaries and American rule. According to Edward Keithahn, Shakes VI was one chief whose power was considerably reduced by the freeing of slaves. Shakes VI lies in state with his regalia in his house in this image from 1916. Local photographer John Worden was often called upon to make a pictorial record of a death. The arrangements, expenses, and gifts for Shakes VI's funeral were paid, according to tradition, by his nephew Charlie Jones. Much of the regalia was sold, including the island itself, by George Shakes's wife, Mary, in 1935. According to Tlingit custom, Jones should have been the next heir, but modern law took precedence this time. After lengthy litigation, the island was turned over to the US Forest Service, and today, the Wrangell Cooperative Association holds it in trust. (Courtesy of the WM.)

This photograph of an unidentified Chinese laborer dates from about 1911. For many years, the colorful Captain Jinks was Wrangell's only Chinese resident. He had come to Wrangell in 1903 to work in the Alaska Packers Association cannery and stayed. He owned a store in the former Wilcox Automotive building (the former Jitterbugs) and sold fireworks and Chinese food. (Photograph by Fred W. Cheney; courtesy of the WM.)

The location of the border between the United States and Canada had long been disputed and moved a number of times, but beginning in 1903, a cooperative effort began to determine the boundary. Work on the Stikine River portion began the next year. The entire survey was not completed until 1914. Pictured are a group of Canadian surveyors and local residents. (Courtesy of MCN.)

Seen here are members of the First Christian Endeavor, a social and religious group affiliated with the Presbyterian Church. The Wrangell group, founded in 1898, had a game room with checkers and dominos and a hall for gymnastics, bowling, and social gatherings. The Rev. Robert Diven also conducted a Christian Endeavor camp for boys and girls at Anan Creek during the 1920s. This group, posed in front of the Presbyterian Church in 1902 for a convention, was composed of delegates from Howkan, Klawock, Klinquan, and Klukquan and included the Howkan Christian Endeavor Band. This was the first such gathering held in Alaska. Rev. Henry P. Corser, at that time a Presbyterian, and later an Episcopalian clergyman, is standing on the far right. In both churches, services were conducted in English and Tlingit for many years until English became the primary language. (Courtesy of the WM.)

The dining room of the Fort Wrangel Hotel must have often been filled with diners such as this merry group of gentlemen. Hiram D. Campbell built the hotel, as well as the Patenaude building (Millie's), the Presbyterian manse, and the Richard and Barbara Angerman and Emde houses, among many others. Rufus Sylvester and Robert Reid had the hotel built, then sold it to John G. Grant. The 1906 fire destroyed the building, but Grant rebuilt it the following year. Below, John G. Grant is pictured at center with unidentified guests in what is probably the family apartment in the hotel. Grant arrived here in 1898 and started a coal business, gradually acquiring considerable property. (Both courtesy of the WM.)

Besides selling general merchandise, Charles Benjamin was a fur buyer. He poses here in 1916 with trappers F.E. Shangle, one of three brothers who trapped on the Iskut (spelled Iskoot at this time) River, and the Burch brothers, William and Frank. Benjamin was elected to the Alaska House of Representatives of the Territory in 1925 and 1927 and to the Alaska Senate in 1929. (Courtesy of the WM.)

Charles Benjamin took many photographs of his son Lloyd "helping" with the family business. Pictured here in about 1914, young Lloyd pushes a cart along the rails of the McCormack Dock across Front Street from the family store. The rails made moving freight from the docked steamers to Front Street businesses easier in the days before trucks. (Photograph by Charles Benjamin; courtesy of Bryant Benjamin.)

These children are standing in Cow Alley. Behind them is St. Rose of Lima Catholic Church and, in the distance, the original Presbyterian manse. From left to right, the children are Joe Prescott, Buster Coulter, Ellery Carlson, Joye Livesay, John Grant, and Erma Grant. The back of this postcard reads, "everywhere board walks." Exploring under Front Street boardwalks was a favorite activity of Wrangell's children, especially on Mondays. They hunted for coins and flasks of bootleg liquor discarded by weekend revelers. Millie Grant recalls that the flasks could be sold for 5¢ each. Below, Homer Worden, son of John Worden, sits with his dog in this photograph from around 1912. (Below, photograph by John E. Worden; courtesy of the WM.)

Photographer John Worden came to Wrangell in 1898 and established the short-lived Fort Wrangel Fish Curing Company across from the sawmill. He then served as postmaster and city clerk while taking many fine photographs of Wrangell. On New Year's Day in 1914, he assembled a group of townspeople in front of the Customs House for this tongue-in-cheek statement about Southeast Alaska's climate: "Get out of the Eastern blizzard zone and locate in S.E. Alaska." The thermometer registered a balmy 38 degrees that day. Several individuals can be identified here, including John G. and Mary Grant on the far right, second row, and future Alaska Native activist Tillie Paul Tamaree in the same row wearing a dark sweater. The Civic Club lobbied unsuccessfully to save the Customs House when the new federal building was being planned in 1939. The building was moved by raft to the old Standard Oil site near Petroglyph Beach (Bangeman's Woods). Children playing with matches set it ablaze, resulting in a total loss. (Photograph by John E. Worden; courtesy of the WM.)

These women are selling moccasins and beadwork. Among the Tlingit, moccasins were worn principally by women, but also by men with snowshoes. The best were made of caribou or moose hide. They were originally plain, but with the availability of beads, the tongues became decorated. Women also sold grass mats, baskets, carving tools, and handmade fishhooks. The Sanitary Packing Cannery, left rear, dates this photograph after 1912. (Photograph by FLP; courtesy of MCN.)

The man in this image may be Charles Gunnuk or Johnny Kassunk. A story about Gunnuk claims that he learned silver carving from the Nass Indians and was the first silver carver in Wrangell. He is mentioned in Emmons as one of only four silver carvers in Alaska in 1882. Silver was obtained from coins and fashioned into wide bracelets for Native use and narrow ones for tourists. (Photographs courtesy of MCN.)

Pictured here are members of the Merlin Elmer Palmer branch of the American Legion, named after a Wrangell man who died in World War I. The Wrangell legion was founded in 1919. On Memorial Day in 1921, these men posed in front of the Red Men's Hall. They are, from left to right, (first row) Andrew Hansen, Steve Grant, unidentified, and Nick Nussbaumer; (second row) Mac McLaughlin, Leonard Campbell, William Taylor, Matt Pellincu, Dr. Hughes, George Sylvester, Ernest Campbell, Fred Lewis, and Louis Scribner; (third row) Charles Moore, unidentified, Elroy Carlson, George Barnes, Harry Coulter, Chet Lloyd, and Laurence Taylor. Besides enlisted men who were sent to Fort William H. Seward in Haines for initial training, Wrangell had enthusiastically organized a Home Guard in March 1917 with 117 members. The first to sign up was pioneer Fred Lynch, age 82. (Courtesy of the WM.)

Pres. Warren G. Harding (to the right of the Naval attaché) visited Wrangell on July 8, 1923, on his way north to drive the last spike in the Alaska Railroad and view conditions in the North. Secretary of Commerce Herbert Hoover is speaking in front of the federal courthouse. Harding fell ill and died on August 2. Suggested causes included food poisoning from Alaska crab, stroke, murder, and suicide. (Courtesy of MCN.)

In 1921, Rev. S. Hall Young returned to Wrangell to gather material for a new book. Pictured here on the beach are, from left to right, (first row) Commissioner of Education Lester Henderson and James W. Pritchett, editor of the *Wrangell Sentinel*; (second row) boat builder William "Chief" Fletcher, community leader Helene Johnson, Rev. S. Hall Young, Sarah Pritchett, and Mrs. Henderson. (Courtesy of the WM.)

The Improved Order of Red Men was a national fraternal organization established in 1849 with rituals modeled after those of Alaska Natives. They were organized into tribes with Wrangell's being the Stikine Tribe. In the photograph above, the tribe's members pose in front of their hall embellished with faux totems in 1921. Pictured from left to right are (first row) Leonard M. Churchill, Ora Brown, Hiram D. Campbell, Patrick C. McCormack, George Barnes, and unidentified; (second row) Alex Vreatt, unidentified, Ed Lindeman, Sam Cunningham, unidentified, ? Cooper, and Ole Johnson; (third row) Charles Benjamin, W. Demmart, Dave Lewis, William B. Lewis, Arnt Sorset, James W. Pritchett, and Mac Mclaughlin; (fourth row) Donald Sinclair, unidentified, Fred Gingrass, Oscar Carlson, Matt Pellincu, unidentified, and Cassius Coulter. (Courtesy of the WM.)

Above is a group of Wrangell's pioneers in the 1930s. From left to right are Thomas J. Case, Emma Baronovich Case, Leonard M. Churchill, and Judge William Thomas. The Cases arrived in 1898 and set up business. Case was the town's first magistrate. Churchill arrived in 1897 and owned a general merchandise store and mail boat. Thomas also arrived in 1897 and served as US marshall and US commissioner. He was married to Lyda McAvoy, a teacher in the first Presbyterian school. Below is Earl West. He came to Wrangell in 1901 and logged, trapped, fished, and served as town marshall. In 1934, he retired to a small cabin in the cove that bears his name. He is remembered for his poetry and sense of humor. (Courtesy of the WM.)

In 1942, the Wrangell Institute was a temporary home for some 200 Aleuts evacuated in response to Japanese aggression in the Aleutian Islands. They were housed in tents on the institute campus before moving to the former Burnett Inlet Salmon Company and Ward Cove for the duration of the war. "Too many trees and no wind," one remarked. Some Aleuts remained in Wrangell after the war. (Courtesy of the WM.)

Pictured here in about 1937 are four Tlingit carvers holding their adzes. These men worked as part of a 30-man Civilian Conservation Corps crew to recreate totems and the tribal house on Shakes Island. From left to right are Joe Thomas, George Collins, Charlie Jones (whose title was Shakes VII), and William Tamaree. (Courtesy of the WM.)

Gathered in front of the Alaska Native Brotherhood (ANB) Hall in 1946 are members of the Alaska Native Sisterhood. They are, from left to right, Nellie Miller, unidentified, Bessie McCullough, unidentified, Mable Willard, Clara Austin, Lucinda Sprat, Louise Bradley, Matilda Tamaree, two unidentified, Anna Person, Nellie Miller, and Susie Jones. The hall was situated to the right of today's Stikine Native Organization (SNO) building. It burned in 1972. (Courtesy of the WM.)

Following the dedication of the Shakes House on June 3, 1940, guests proceeded to the ANB Hall for what was called "the last great potlatch" and the naming of Chief Shakes VII. During this ceremony, the histories of the clan were retold. Seen here are the guests, including Susie Jones (center front, in regalia), as they troop down Front Street from the Shakes House to the Hall. (Photograph by Otto C. Schallerer; courtesy of Greg McCormack.)

All of Wrangell, as well as about 1,500 guests from out of town, gathered on June 3, 1940, to celebrate the completion of a traditional Tlingit clan house on Shakes Island. The ceremony began with a 50-foot war canoe approaching the island, manned by Natives dressed in regalia, singing and chanting. Upon reaching the island, Charlie Jones, soon to be Chief Shakes VII, stepped out and received the welcome of the people. Many decisions about the house's reconstruction were left to the Tlingit carvers and builders. In preparation, Tom Ukas built a scale model. The finished structure incorporates many of the elders' memories of the components of a classic Tlingit house. Two Kadashan totems and two new poles were also carved for this project. Today, the house is used for Native ceremonies and to educate visitors about traditional Tlingit life. Seven decades of Southeast Alaska's damp climate have made it necessary to plan for replacing rotting beams and the roof in the near future. (Courtesy of the WM.)

Nine

PANORAMAS

Mount Dewey modestly rises on the north end of Wrangell. From the town's inception, it attracted those who wanted a panoramic view of the town and its setting. John Muir famously climbed the hill one stormy night in 1879, built a roaring bonfire, and gloried in the raging winds. The Tlingit below were not only puzzled by the mysterious blaze on the hilltop, but also by the enigmatic man who set it afire. Muir took no photographs, more is the pity, but since that day, photographers, both professional and amateur, have climbed the hill and left a record of Wrangell through the years. Later photographers documented Wrangell from the air.

In the earliest panorama, taken around 1889, Wrangell looks strangely meager, but the difference in the second photograph is clear. The Klondike rush has come and gone, but it left behind a village burgeoning with new stores, homes, and businesses. From now on, the waterfront will continually change, adding a wharf, a breakwater, new accommodations for ships, and seafood processors.

The presence and configuration of landmark buildings help locate these images in time. Changes in the fort, the presence of St. Rose of Lima (missing between 1898 and 1909), the shape of the Presbyterian Church before and after the 1930 fire, the Bishop Rowe Hospital built in 1926, and the new school in 1931 all provide clues as to when the photographer ascended the hill or boarded a plane.

One constant, thus far, has been the shape and beauty of the mountains and waterways in which Wrangell is set. Looking out to the Elephant's Nose or south over Zimovia Strait, an observer can delight in the same vistas as Wrangell ancestors enjoyed nearly 200 years ago. Trees still cloak the hills, salmon fills the streams, and people stroll the streets smiling or scowling as their nature dictates. Both change and permanence are part of the telling of Wrangell's story.

This early view from a Mount Dewey still denuded of trees from the fort's construction and firewood needs, dates from around 1889. Wrangell has suffered through the booms and busts of the fur trade and two gold rushes. A third rush, the Klondike, swamped the town with prospectors from around the world for a brief period during 1897 and 1898. The Willson and Sylvester sawmill, constructed in 1889 and backed by the Kadashan house, is visible in the middle distance. On the far peninsula is the cluster of houses of the Shustak clan. Other Tlingit clan houses line the curving shoreline. The first St. Rose of Lima Catholic Church, whose walls appear braced, is visible here. The original Presbyterian Church and the manse with fenced yard sit on the far left. The fort's blockhouse still stands at right, next to the hip-roofed fort hospital/school, and the Fort Wrangel Hotel is yet to be built. On Front Street, there are only stores on the upland side. (Courtesy of MCN.)

This photograph was taken around 1900, when Mount Dewey was partially cleared and an observation shelter was built for picnics. A cold storage plant, the Wrangell Dock and Cold Storage Company, has displaced the three-story Greif brewery and the company has added a new wharf, at center. A boardwalk built in 1903 connects the town's business district, which now boasts buildings on both sides of the street. Residences are beginning to dot the slope of Mount Dewey, and streetlights will be installed in 1905. The landmark turreted Fort Wrangel Hotel is on the far right. The Reid and Sylvester dock behind the hotel has been widened, and a warehouse has been added to handle the increasing freight traffic. Three floating canneries were operating during this period. One sternwheeler is moored to the central wharf, while three others sit in the Inner Harbor area, left rear, and a fourth rests on the beach, as seen on the left. The town is still named Fort Wrangel and will not be called simply "Wrangell" until 1903. (Photograph by Frank LaRoche; courtesy of MCN.)

This photograph in 1914 illustrates some of the changes on Front Street following the 1906 fire. The Wrangell Hotel is rebuilt but only two stories high, and the Patenaude building, erected in 1906, can be seen on the lower right. The newly finished St. Rose of Lima Church stands in the lower center of the image. A few years later, four steamship lines will be bringing ships to the McCormack Dock, far left center, where only a decade earlier Stikine River paddle wheelers had crowded. Small boats are anchored in the harbor, but the inner harbor will not be dredged until 1936. A map drawn this year by the Sanborn Fire Insurance Company shows only a handful of streets but includes Front, Church, Stikine, Fort, Cassiar, McKinnon, Episcopal, and Greif Streets, and Cow Alley. Substantial new homes are beginning to appear on Church Street. During World War I, a local group trims one of the tallest trees on Mount Dewey and attaches a pulley and rope to display the American flag. (Photograph by John E. Worden; courtesy of Leonard and Lynne Campbell.)

By the early 1930s, some additions had been made to the waterfront. A breakwater extending from Shustak Point was built in 1925, and the next year, a city float inside the breakwater was installed. Floating shrimp, crab, and salmon canneries stationed themselves in the harbor anchored off of Shakes Point. The inner harbor has been dredged in this photograph, making room for a small boat shelter and boat shops. The Wrangell Packing Company has constructed a cannery on the sawmill wharf. Roads are stretching both north and south of town, beginning with a road from the head of the bay to the cemetery in 1918. In 1930, a road to Shoemaker Bay was established, and during the next year, a road replaced the footpath to the Alaska Packer's Association cannery at Point Highfield. A cold storage and shrimp cannery have been added to the McCormack Dock, and a third story, added in 1924, sits atop the Wrangell Hotel. (Photograph by Mabel or Emil Fisher; courtesy of MCN.)

Wrangell began to get regular air service when airmail delivery began in 1928. This aerial photograph from the early 1930s shows the new public school, finished in 1931. To the left of the school is the Presbyterian Church as it appears today after fire destroyed the original building in 1930. On the far left, the old courthouse still stands, not to be replaced until 1941 with the new federal building. Two steamship docks are on the far left. The sawmill appears to be inactive at the time of this photograph (note the A-frame logging apparatus tied to the dock) but the Wrangell Packing Company, seen at the end of the mill dock, is in business. The white Bishop Rowe Hospital with two dormers is visible at center right. In 1928, the northern addition to Wrangell was added, enlarging the town site as far as the Standard Oil plant, which is next to today's Petroglyph Beach and is now called Bangeman's Woods. (Courtesy of the WM.)

By 1943, Wrangell had weekly air service to Ketchikan and Juneau with Ellis Air and Alaska Coastal Airways. Beside the McCormack Dock, with a steamship in port on the day this image was captured, is the Canadian National Steamship Company dock. To its left is the federal building. The Customs House and small building to its left used by the American Legion are all that remain of old Fort Wrangell. A plank street runs north (left) toward the Diamond K Packing Company. The seawall along Stikine Avenue would not be built until 1945. The pilings on which rest much of Front Street, making the town vulnerable to fire, are much in evidence in this photograph. Wrangell's population is about 1,200 in 1941. Three salmon canneries, a shrimp and crab cannery, and a cold storage all were operating in the early 1940s. Wrangell's economy struggled during World War II without the boom of wartime construction, but several new industries kept the economy afloat. (Courtesy of the WM.)

BIBLIOGRAPHY

Andrews, Clarence L. *Wrangell and the Gold of the Cassiar*. Seattle, WA: Luke Tinker, 1937.

Cohen, Kathryn. *Wrangell Historic Building Survey and Inventory*. Wrangell, AK: Phoenix Associates, 1986.

Corser, Henry Prosper. *Totem Lore of the Alaska Indian and the Land of the Totem*. Wrangell, AK: Walter C. Waters, n.d.

DeMuth, Phyllis and Michael Sullivan. *A Guide to the Alaska Packer's Association Records, 1891–1970 in the Alaska Historical Library*. Juneau, AK: Alaska Department of Education, Division of State Libraries and Museums, 1983.

Emmons, George Thornton. *The Tlingit Indians*. Frederica de Laguna, ed. Seattle, WA: University of Washington Press, 1990.

Herem, Barry. "In the Shadow of the Wrangell Master." *American Indian Art Magazine*. Autumn 1994, pp. 74–85.

Keithahn, Edward L. *The Authentic History of Shakes Island and Clan*. Wrangell, AK: Wrangell Historical Society, 1981.

Kiffer, Dave. "Seward was one of Alaska's first tourists (A history of Alaska tourism, part 1)." Stories in the News. www.sitnews.us, July 12, 2010.

Keithahn, Edward L. *Monuments in Cedar: The Authentic Story of the Totem Pole*. New York: Bonanza Books, 1963.

Miller, Polly and Leon Gordon Miller. *Lost Heritage of Alaska*. New York: Bonanza Books, 1967.

Neal, Patricia. *Wrangell, Alaska: Gateway to the Stikine River, 1834–1899*. Greenwich, CT: Coachlamp Productions, 2007.

Scidmore, Eliza R. *Alaska, Its Southern Coast and the Sitkan Archipelago*. Boston: Lothrop Co., 1885.

Wick, Carol I. *Ocean Harvest*. Seattle, WA: Superior Publishing Co., 1946.

Young, S. Hall. *Hall Young of Alaska*. New York: Fleming H. Revell Co., 1927.

INDEX

Barrington Transportation, 59, 62
Benjamin, Charles, 31, 72, 108, 114
Campbell, Hiram D., 14, 36, 107, 114
Canneries, 8, 15, 16, 48, 50, 51, 56, 57, 60, 65–67, 69–71, 74, 77, 83, 105, 111, 121, 123, 125
Cassiar Gold Rush, 9, 11, 16, 56, 99
Cassiar District, 7, 44, 65,78
Chief Shakes V (Kow-ish-te), 86, 87, 92
Chief Shakes VI (Gush-klin), 30, 87, 94, 103
Chief Shakes VII (Charlie Jones, Kudanake), 96, 101, 116, 117, 118
Churchill, Leonard M., 60, 114, 115
Corser, Rev. Henry P., 37, 79, 85, 90, 102, 106
Doctors, 27, 49
Fire Department, 21, 24, 32, 82
Fires, 8, 13, 15, 17, 21, 26, 31, 33–34, 63, 71, 79, 80, 98, 107, 119, 122, 124
Fishing, 8, 29, 39, 53, 61, 65, 66, 68–70, 74, 99
Fort Wrangel, 2, 8, 9–14, 15, 16, 18, 100
Fort Wrangel Hotel, 21, 26, 107, 120, 121
Furs, 7, 30, 46, 65, 76, 85, 99, 108, 120
Grant, John G., 21, 22, 46, 47, 107, 109, 110
Greif, Bruno, 19, 20, 23, 80
Hospitals, 11, 12, 14, 20, 27, 35, 39, 44, 63, 119, 120, 124
Hudson's Bay Company, 7, 11, 22, 59
Kadashan, John, 73, 79, 90, 102
Kiks.adi, 89, 94, 96
Klondike Gold Rush, 8, 9, 12, 18, 22, 58, 99, 119, 120
Lear, William "King," 9, 11, 54
Lemieux, Antine, 23, 47
Logging, 31, 51, 56, 65, 72, 79, 103, 115, 124
Matheson, Farquahar, 22, 53, 95
McCormack Dock, 13, 22, 28, 34, 54, 63, 70, 84, 95, 108, 122, 123, 125
McCormack family, 32, 54, 98, 114

McFarland, Amanda, 35, 39, 101
Mining, 8, 16, 51, 58, 65, 74, 77, 78, 99
Nolan, James, 27, 82
Paddle wheelers, 51, 58, 122
Patenaude, Leo, 26
Post Offices, 22, 28, 45, 46, 94
Presbyterian Church, 18, 19, 35, 36, 39, 41, 63, 77, 106, 119, 120, 124
Red Men, Improved Order, 20, 33, 112, 114
Russians, 7, 9, 10, 76, 79, 90, 93, 99, 103
St. Rose of Lima Catholic Church, 37, 109, 119, 120, 122
Salvation Army, 35, 38, 46
Sawmill, 2, 8, 16, 19, 28, 46, 48, 63, 71, 72, 73, 74, 84, 90, 99, 103, 110, 123, 124
Schools, 9, 11, 12, 13, 14, 35, 39–43, 49, 83, 95, 101, 115, 119, 120, 124
Shakes House, 2, 85, 87, 92, 98, 99, 117, 118
Sinclair, Donald, 25, 114
Steamships, 13, 28, 47, 51, 54, 55, 98, 122, 124, 125
Stikine Gold Rush, 7, 58, 76
Stikine River, 7, 8, 9, 18, 51, 58, 68, 71, 75, 77, 89, 100, 102, 105, 122
Sylvester, Rufus, 12, 46, 54, 74, 83, 107
Telegraph Creek, 7, 51, 53, 58, 59, 78, 99
Tourism, 8, 16, 18, 23, 26, 51, 52, 55, 84, 90, 92, 94, 100, 111
United States Army, 8, 9, 11, 12, 29, 39
Waters, Walter, 30, 54, 60, 98
Willson, Thomas A., 46, 74
Worden, John E., 2, 6, 14, 21, 36, 47, 57, 58, 61, 66, 67, 74, 76, 84, 92, 94, 101, 104, 107, 109, 110, 122
Wrangell, Ferdinand von, 9
Wrangell Institute, 43, 116
Young, S. Hall, 35, 102, 113

Visit us at
arcadiapublishing.com

CPSIA information can be obtained
at www.ICGtesting.com
Printed in the USA
LVHW06*0252100418
572902LV00012B/25/P